The Skateboarding Bible

2022:
+ 36 PAGES
+ 12 TRICKS

Learn, progress and innovate, with over 72 detailed step-by-step skate tricks.

Tant Maxime

The skateboarding bible

Learn about the world of skateboarding, it's history, how to progress and innovate.

Maxime Tant

Summary

Before the adventure starts

A word from the author

How to read this book

Introduction

About QR codes

<u>Part I :</u> The history of skateboarding

<u>Part II :</u> The world of skateboarding

<u>Part III :</u> The different skaters

<u>Part IV :</u> Before hopping on to your board

- Anatomy of skateboarding
- Equipment
- Muscle warm-up and stretching
- Stretching after the session
- Injuries: prevention and first aid

Knowing your stance

Fakie, nollie, switch? What is that ?

Knowing how to ride and to turn

<u>Tricks section :</u>

- Flat (Ground Tricks)
- Ramps Tricks
- Grinds & Slides
- The Grabs
- Special Tricks and Old School

Annex 1 : Choosing your board   Annex 2 : Game of Skate

Annex 3 : Having your own style or following one?   Annex 4 : The rider section

Annex 5: Jumping higher and improving the height of your tricks, is it possible?

Annex 6 : About the author   Annex 7 : A few cool links

Annex 8: Skate Tricks App and Blog   Annex 9 : Glossary

Before the adventure starts

To you who are reading this book, welcome. I hope that you'll appreciate it and it will enable you to discover skateboarding or to help you with your progress.

Caution: Skateboarding has existed for many years, however it's not without its risks. And so, it's up to you to protect yourself and try tricks at your own risk and peril, we are in no way responsible in case of an accident. Remember to warm up a bit, this will improve your sessions and will give you the confidence to try new tricks. Be careful, move forward step by step at your own pace if you want to avoid any injuries.

Thanks: Many people have lent their knowledge for the writing of this book. That's why all these people deserve to have their names written below. A book cannot be written with just the snap of a finger, it needs time and organization. So thank you, those who helped and supported me for the writing of this book, thanks to you skateboarding will continue to persist throughout the years!

Photographe : Alexandre Gbt.
Skaters : Alex, Hugues, Bigz, André.
Translation : Danielle.H

And of course you, who is reading this book at this very moment!

Hey you ! Be sure to follow me on my Instagram : @tantmaxime or https://www.instagram.com/tantmaxime/

A word from the author

I've been skateboarding since I was 16. Like many I discovered it thanks to a friend who taught me the basics. As I progressed I always wanted to go further, however there were only a few skaters in my town and so my skating stopped improving.

We would use the internet to look up American tips or tricks on YouTube. This helped a bit to do new tricks, but it doesn't compare to the advice given from French speakers for French speakers.

It's as if you were given a recipe but without the measurements, you wouldn't really know how to measure out the ingredients. It's the same for skateboarding as there are a number of steps to do one after the other in order to do a trick: foot placement, bending of the knees, the gap, the pop and not to mention all the other parameters.

If we compare skateboarding to any other practice, we can quickly acknowledge that, unfortunately, there isn't much learning material.

That's how I'll make a dream come true, for who I was at 16 and for those who skate: this book is in your hands so don't hesitate to share it with your friends and, of course, open it up to discover it step by step.

How to read this book ?

As you'll be learning to skate with the help of this book, and in parallel practice (I hope), I would advise you to start by reading all the basics of skateboarding, by that I mean the first few presentation pages of this book and the practice of skateboarding followed up with the next tricks:

- Ollie
- Nollie
- Ollie 180°
- Shove-it
- Kickflip and/or Heelflip

For me these are the basic tricks that you need, after that you'll be free to change it up and, for example, use the ramp (rock, feeble, axle stall...) grinds (50-50, crook..), slides etc.

Do what you feel is best, however I do recommend learning the bare minimum to properly familiarize yourself with skateboarding.

Important note: I sorted the tricks by order of difficulty myself. For example with the flat (floor tricks), this starts with the Ollie, the ramp starts with the drop, the grind with the 50-50 etc. Everything has been done to ensure you have a good progression, so try to respect the order of the book if you wish to progress quicker.

Introduction

If you are currently reading this then it means that you're already passionate about skateboarding. Or that you dream about skateboarding but you don't even own one.

This guide is here to help loosen your inflamed tibias after a little session with your friends, to pass the time in the toilets, at the beach or even during math or history. We'll keep that one to ourselves.

Through these pages, written by skaters for skaters, you'll learn the flat, grinds, the ramp, how to be the king of the skateboarding game, to innovate and finally, most importantly, having fun on your board and enjoying it while doing so.

Skateboarding is a world far more vast than we think, with various types of people from different backgrounds. That's the beauty of it. Moreover there are absolutely no rules which also means no limits. Each skater is free to do as he pleases, to create his tricks, modules, to film...

This book will teach beginners, as well as confirmed skaters, the nearly full amount of existing skateboarding tricks to this day.

Not wanting to do things halfway, and being truly passionate about skateboarding, I've pushed this book as far as I can to teach you to skate as best I can.

Unfortunately I won't be there with you to teach you how to do your first ollie or laser flip, but you must know that skateboarding is a long term adventure.

The more you'll persevere, the more you'll find pleasure by expanding your panel of tricks.

Skateboarding is vast and completely open and free, that's why it will continue to persevere throughout the years, even when they'll be hoverboards, we'll still be able to do tricks!

Have a good time reading this book!

M.T

About QR codes

As you may have already noticed if you flipped through the pages, there is a QR code per trick, and on some other pages. These are very useful during your training, as they bring an additional support to this book: the video!

To make it simple:

1- Get yourself an app that's used for scanning QR codes, if you don't already have one, there are plenty on Play store and Apple store.

2- Open the app

3- Scan the QR code as if you were photographing a beautiful monument

4- Make the most of the additional content

All of the videos were selected by me, and I chose them based on two simple criteria: the image quality and the speed. Most of them are in slow motion, which enables you to really see how every trick is done.

You can test it with this one:

Part 1

The history of skateboarding

1930: Children create scooters using a little wooden crate and a little piece of wood to make the handlebar. Little by little they remove the handlebar to use it only with their feet. And so skateboarding was born.

1950: If you've seen the film "Lords of Dogtown" the history is well presented. It's in 1950 that skateboarding really takes on its name, with the marketing of the first models of the "roll-surf" thanks to the invention from surfers who wanted to continue to train in the streets in order to have a semblance of surfing on a concrete surface.

1959: The brand Roller Derby sees the light of day and markets a completely revised model, especially with the design of the board.

1960-1970: Skateboarding arrives in France and skateparks start to be built in the US. The practice is democratized and millions of skateboards are sold across the world, magazines on the practice start to become known.

1963: First skateboarding advert in a surf magazine.

1966: Creation of the iconic brand Vans.

1972: Appearance of urethane wheels: the skater can ride faster and longer.

1978: The legendary Alan Gelfand revolutionizes skateboarding by inventing the Ollie.

1980 to 1990: Skateboarding changes, names like Natas Kaupas or even Rodney Mullen revolutionize skateboarding by creating tricks such as flips. The usage of railings is democratized in the skateboarding field. Skaters are skateboarding in the streets more than in skateparks.

1981: The first volumes of Thrasher Magazine are published.

1992: Appearance of the switch by Salman Agah.

1999: Release of the legendary Tony Hawk's Pro skater game which will then launch a series of video games. To finish 1999, Tony Hawk entered the first 900 ° in the world.

2004: Danny Way performs the longest ramp jump: 24 meters.

2005: Release of the legendary film: "The Lords of Dogtown" telling the story of the beginning of skateboarding in 1950 with the Z-boys including Stacy Peralta, Tony Alva and Jay Adams. These people are now legendary in the world of skateboarding.

2007: Release of the video game EA Skate, more oriented towards simulation than Tony Hawks' Pro Skater. The second one was released in 2008 and the last one (Skate 3) in 2010. Many skaters (myself included) are still waiting for Skate 4.

2007 (yes again): Rob Dyrdek enters the longest boardslide in the world: 30.62 meters!

2008: Creation of the Battle of the Berrics, the skating game between pro skaters on YouTube. Zach Kral sets the record for the number of consecutive kickflips which is now 1546. And no, it's not a typo.

2009: Rob Dyrdek and Joe Ciaglia unveiled the most impressive skateboard in history. Dimensions: 11.14 meters long, 2.63 meters wide and 1.1 meters high, which is 12.5 x bigger than a classic skate! Chris Cole wins the second edition of Battle At The Berrics.
Release of the film Street Dreams with Paul Rodriguez, Terry Kennedy, Rob Dyrdek, Ryan Sheckler as well as Ryan Dunn of the Jackass.

2010: Creation of the Street League Skateboarding competition by Rob Dyrdek, the winner of the competition will cash in 100 000 $. It's without a doubt the biggest Skateboarding competition across the world where the best skaters go up against each other. The competition is renewed each year. Paul Rodriguez wins the third edition of the Battle At The Berrics.

2011: One of the most striking records was broken which pushes the limits: the tallest ollie on flatground, by Aldrin Garcia with his 114 centimeters high! Morgan Smith wins the fourth annual Battle At The Berrics.

2012: Thirteen-year-old Tom Schaar defeats Tony Hawk with the first 1080 ° in history on the board. P.J Ladd wins the fifth annual Battle At The Berrics.

2013: P.J Ladd wins the sixth annual Battle At The Berrics. He is the only one to have won two editions of Battle At The Berrics. To know that the level is high, the difficulty of the tricks in flat rises quickly, and the consistency of the skaters in the success of the tricks is really impressive to see year after year.

2014: Cody Cepeda wins the seventh edition of Battle At The Berrics.

2015: Sewa Kroetkov wins the eighth edition of Battle At The Berrics.

2016: Skateboarding has been accepted for the first time as a sport for the 2020 Tokyo Olympics. Aaron Homoki goes over the legendary gap of the 25 steps of Lyon. Diego Najera wins the ninth edition of the Battle At The Berrics.

2017: 143 kilometers per hour. It's Kyle Westler's world record for the fastest downhill in history. It was of course done on a longboard, but I thought it would be nice to show you that a skate can go faster than a car and have no fines and without consuming any resources. Chris Joslin wins the tenth edition of the Battle At The Berrics.

2018: Back-to-back Ollie world record (308) by American Nicholas Drachman. Luan Oliveira wins the eleventh edition of the Battle At The Berrics. Actor Jonah Hill goes behind the camera to release his first (and excellent) 90's feature film, a film about the adventure of a young teenager, his relationship with skateboarding and his difficult life.

2019: Monica Torres wins the inaugural Women's Battle At The Berrics. There is no male winner, as this year has been reserved for the female contest only.

2020: Due to the pandemic, a special edition called Battle at The Berrics Quarantine has been created, Seirra Fellers will win this edition.

2021: Skateboarding's first participation in the Olympic Games (postponed to 2021 due to the COVID-19 pandemic). The competition was held in two categories for each gender: park and street. The winners :

> _Men:_ Yuto Horigome (Street) and Keegan Palmer (Park)
> _Women:_ Momiji Nishiya (Street) and Sakura Yosozumi (Park)

The twelfth edition of Battle at The Berrics has been canceled due to the Covid-19 pandemic.

2022: Jamie Griffin wins the twelfth edition of Battle At The Berrics. To know that this edition saw new highly anticipated skaters compete: Aurelien Giraud, Jonny Giger, Mike V (back), Garrett Ginner, Jamie Griffin, Mike Mo (back after his injury), and many more. Surely one of the most impressive and expected seasons, although at the end some skaters were unable to participate in the last rounds due to health/border restrictions, in particular Giger & Giraud who were highly anticipated.

Skate 4 is finally announced, 12 years after Skate 3! At the time of writing this book update, the release date has not been announced but several video recordings of the pre Alpha versions of Skate 4 can be seen on YouTube. Meanwhile there have been more than correct Skater XL and Session.

A few photos of the first skateboards :

The 5 fastest Downhills in history, including Kyle Westler's:

Several of the most impressive records (available in English):

Aaron Homoki and the 25 steps of Lyon:

Part II
The world of skateboarding

Once you're past a certain point in skateboarding, you'll begin to realize that this will be way more than a sport or art to you. To you this will become a way of life and not a hobby like others or something to pass the time like watching TV.

Skateboarding is a world apart, skaters help each other learn new tricks, encourage each other to succeed, construct things together like new spots. That's the skateboarding spirit, it's a true family.

To begin with, most skaters spend about 10 minutes at the skatepark or on a spot. Then time goes by, progression goes up and they'll spend hours and hours until they can't go without it, some skaters will compare it to a drug. I even think that most skaters can't go without riding for a long period of time.

Skateboarding changes life, in a way that it changes your perception of life. Now, for you the main usage of a bench is no longer to sit on it, all you'll see is the magnificent curbs ready to be skated on. As soon as you see steps, or even a rail, your attention will immediately be drawn to it like a pink elephant. You'll develop a whole new vision of your environment, the Skate vision.

The nice steps where you would sit with your friends to chat are now just a magnificent gap where you'll go every Sunday "because there's no one there on Sundays". The big covered supermarket parking lot will no longer be an annoying area to drive through but instead it will be your heaven when it rains in order to do some flat sessions or curbs on the cement edges.

Welcome to the world of skateboarding!

Part III
The different skaters

The lazy guy : He skates for 10 minutes and then talks for the rest of the session. This is the same guy that always comes to talk about his girlfriends, tv shows or his dog. Generally he has a brand new board, his tail and nose are newer than in the skate shop. It's also often him who'll post selfies on a board, or who'll go past with a Thrasher t-shirt.

The crazy guy : This one, you shouldn't ask him to try a trick, because he will do it. It's surely him who'll give you the most amount of motivation. You saw a set of 10 steps that frightened you? That's fine, but he has already gone over them with a laser switch while you're trying your first manuals.

The beginner who wants to get hit: The one that does mini power slides on the inclined plane and who has waxed it like an ice skating rink. The one that will die within a few minutes because the guys on the BMX will fall flat on their faces because of him. It's highly likely that this individual will then convert to riding a scooter.

The "I'll try again next time": The beginners syndrome, you want him to progress, and so does he, but at 50%. After all, better late than never!

The loud mouth: This one has done it all, when you were learning Ollie he was already doing the backflip in LA with Tony Hawk. But in OUT when you do a trick that he's never seen he'll tell you to retry even though it was neat. He'll also fake a call from his girlfriend when he has the T in the skating game.
He's gapped the four blocks at Bercy Paris in Switch Tre with his hands behind his back, easy.

The cameraman: This one films everything, even when you'll go to throw up behind the ramp, he'll post it all over social media. Above everything he loves to film kids that fall from their scooters, or who fall off the rails. He often has a longboard. But of course when you log in a new trick, he didn't film.

Spot-man: The coolest one of the group, he'll find you the biggest spots.

The handyman: He spends more time whacking on things like a maniac than he does on his deck. His bearing life expectancy is weirdly as high as the time he spends on his board.
He's also the guy that'll ask "don't you have a truck to help me out?". He doesn't repair his shoes with glue but with adhesive tape.

The music guy: he is in his own bubble, he always rides with his music. You can't even offer him an OUT he won't hear you, if there's a bomb he doesn't care either, he just wants to ride alone with his music.

The alcohol guy: The only skater you'll never see drinking water whether it be the winter or the summer. He is often accompanied by a large beer pack in his bag. It's normal if at the end of the session he can't do an ollie correctly.

The overly talkative: like Pareto's law, he spends 80% of his time discussing and 20% (if not less) discussing.

NB: this is all humor as you will understand, but I can assure you that you'll come across a few of them.

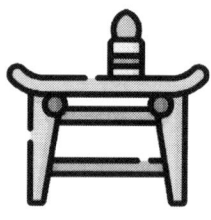

Part IV

Before jumping on your skateboard

Anatomy of the skateboard

The board: The wooden part of the skateboard. The area where you place your feet in order to skate. Many different board dimensions exist depending on your size, for more info I'd advise you to read the "Choosing your board" section.

The grip: The black sticky paper, that we can compare to sand paper. It's used to maintain the grip of the shoes to the board, and to do tricks. Without the grip it's a lot more difficult, you'll have the chance to try one day.

The trucks: They are responsible for holding the wheels but also to lead the board, in particular thanks to the bones. They are held in place by four screws to maintain the truck on the board. We'll also find the kingpin in the center that maintains the bones.

The wheels: A total of four wheels on a skateboard, there are various sizes and materials (see section "choosing your board").

The bearings: They are present on each wheel in pairs, and so a total of 8 bearings by skateboard is necessary. Three categories exist: Abec 3, 5 and 7. The higher the category the faster the bearings will be.

The screws: This is all of the screws used for the skateboard, the 8 screws and their nuts to maintain the truck to the board. You'll also need an Allen key for most of the screws. Skate tools are also useful because all the tools are in one, but it's not every day that you'll need to unscrew your board so this is an optional purchase. In the meantime I would advise that you settle for the good old tools: Allen keys, size 13 socket wrench for most truck kingpins, and 8 or 9 for the screws that maintain the truck.

Kingpin: The screw of consistent size in the truck, it helps to keep it straight with its bones. It often gets damaged on its upper part, especially because of failed ollie grinds when riding in the modules.

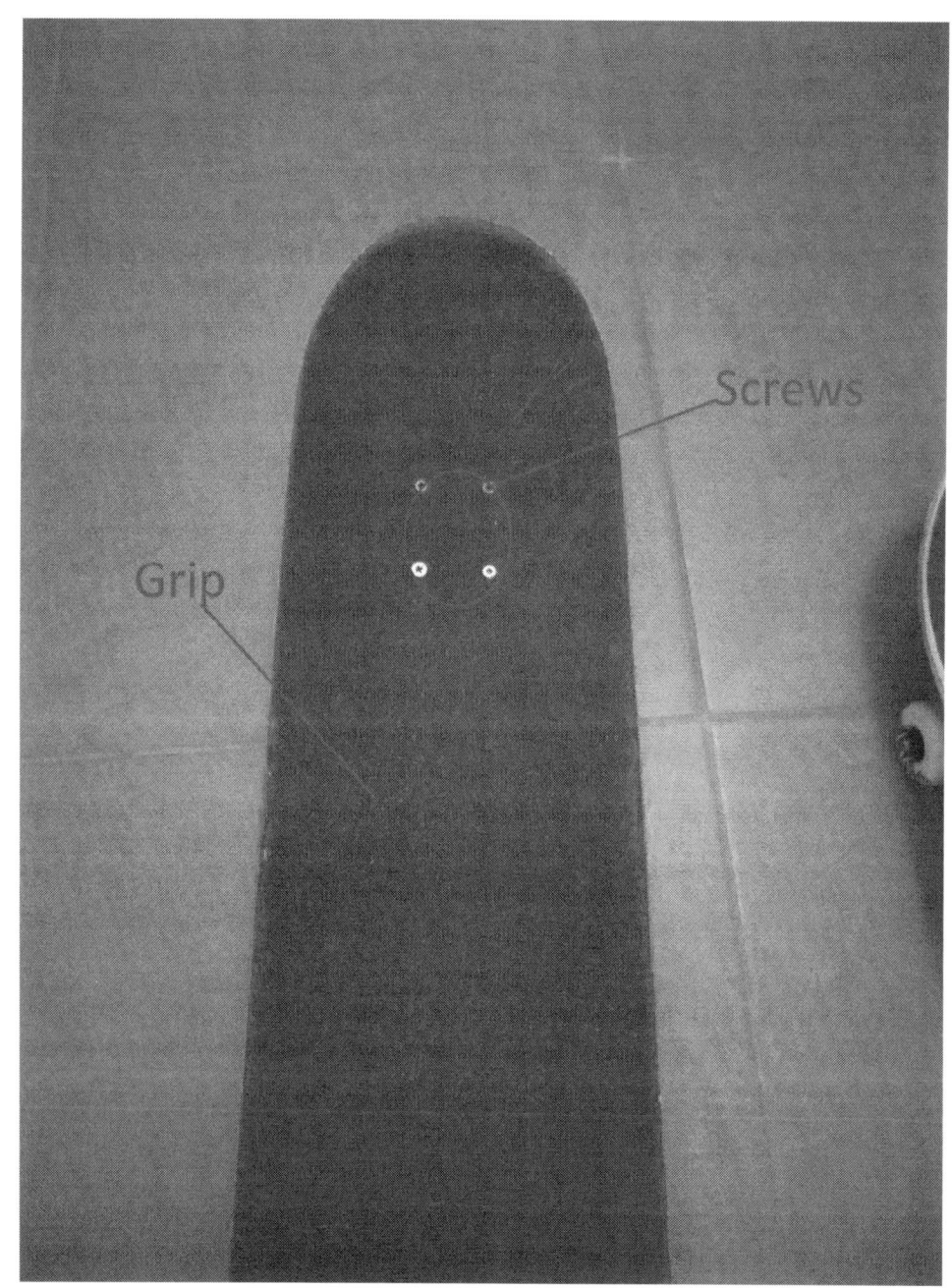

View from above

Rear view

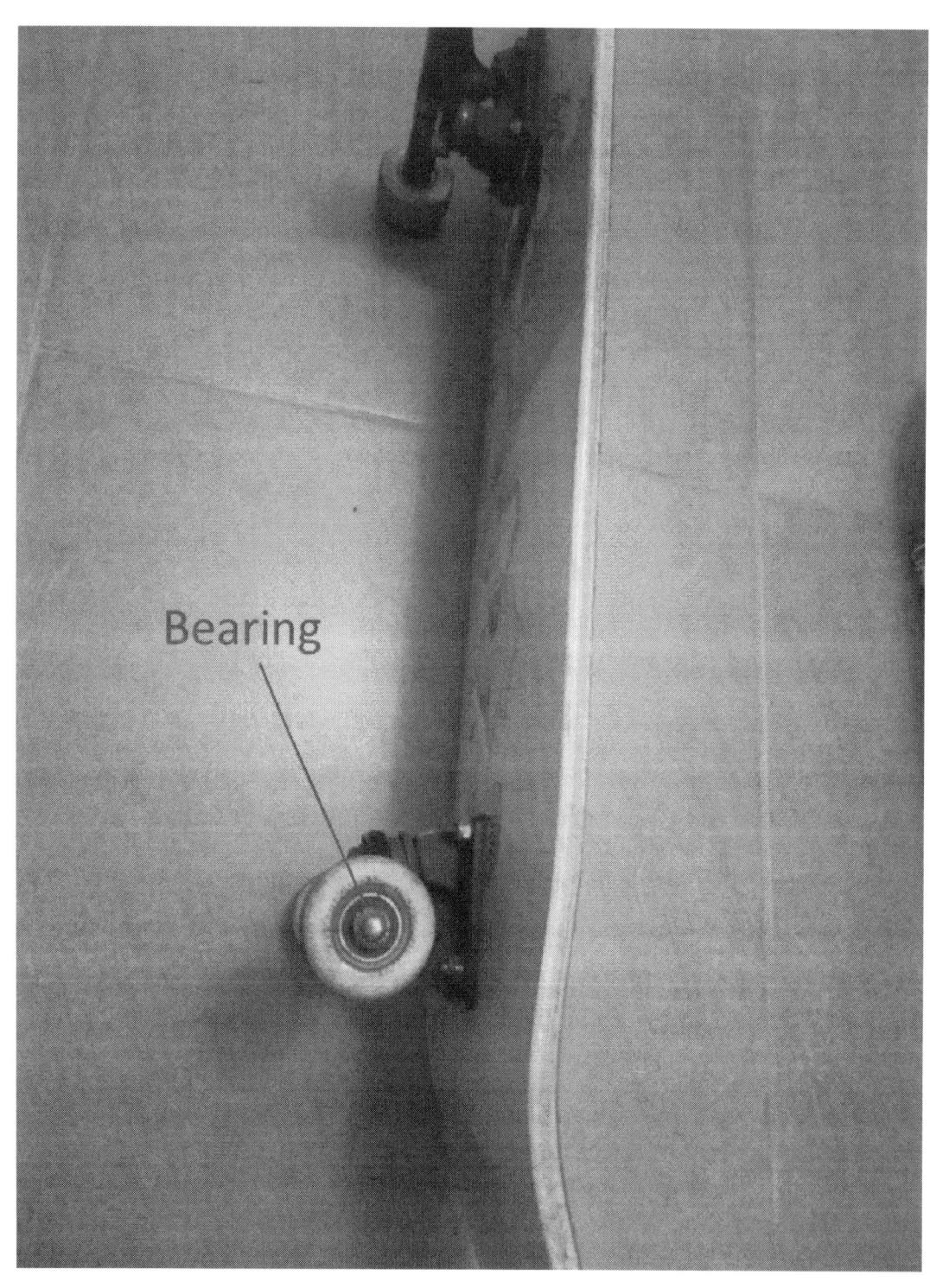

View from the side

Equipment

To skate you don't need too much substantial equipment. That's the advantage of it, because it's also one of the cheapest extreme sports if we compare it to BMX or even freestyle scootering.

In order to skate in good conditions, I would advise that you invest in a low price skateboard that you'll find for less than 30$ in any sports shop.

Why? Simply to know if you really like skateboarding before investing over 100$ in a high end quality board.

The second point, which is as important as the board itself: the shoes!

Shoes are expensive for a skater, simply because each time a trick is done the shoes scrape against the grip. This grip, which is similar to sandpaper, apart from the fact that its base color is black. And so to conclude on the shoes, the wear and tear is a lot higher once you reach a certain level.

You have three choices:

1- Protect the shoes with a special glue that you can find in your local skate shop, or online. This glue will considerably reduce the wear and tear of your shoes but at the cost of the aesthetic. The glue doesn't really give a nice aspect to the shoes (see next photo), however you are skating so for the money that the glue will save you this is the more judicious choice I can advise you!

2- Buy new shoes as soon as a hole appears, if not your socks will pay the price and then your feet.

3 - Buy second-hand shoes on sites like Vinted (it's not a paid investment, I really like the platform). This is in my opinion the best solution. You can find excellent brands like Nike SB, Adidas, Lakai, Emerica... at a lower price compared to overpriced new shoes. The ideal is therefore to take second-hand shoes and protect them.

For beginners we would still advise protections. You have to know that it's at the start of the practice that you'll fall the most! Wearing a helmet at least will insure your safety, the worst falls are the ones on the head. And always go forward bit by bit, don't jump 4 steps if you don't know how to go down a curb whilst doing an ollie!

Knee Pads for skateboarding

A worn out shoe from skateboarding

The importance of the warm-up

      The human body is not a machine, you'll see that for yourself if you skate more than one day in a row. You'll feel weakness in your thighs and stinging in maybe one or even both calves.

These are aches. They appear after a muscular disorder, as your muscles are shocked, your body repairs itself to make it larger and stronger.

It's exactly as if you did weight training.

The targeted muscles by skating are the calves, the quadriceps, the hamstrings and finally the buttocks. If you know a few weight training moves we can compare this to squats.

The trauma is minimal and entirely natural so there is no need to worry.

To avoid all of this the best thing to do is a little warm-up before each session. You should already know these warm-ups as they are the same as what you did in PE.

Meaning: running for a few minutes (1-2 minutes), do a few high knees while running or on the spot, it's up to you, and finally butt kicks, and again either whilst running or on the spot. But most importantly the joints, so if you are too lazy to do a complete warm-up (at your own risk), at least warm-up your knees and ankles.

Execution of the basic joint warm-up:

Stand up and put a hand on a wall, a barrier whatever, just to keep your balance.
Put one of your two feet upright, on the big toe (like the famous dance move).
"Draw" circles with your ankle using the basic big toe to circle. This warm-up warms up the ankle. Repeat the process with your other foot.
Penultimate step: the knees.
Still standing, put your two feet together, lean forward and put your hands on your knees. As for the ankles, we will draw circles to warm up the knees.
For the ankles as for the knees, do not hesitate to change the direction of rotation to optimize the warm-up.
You can make 10 to 20 circles, it will be already very good.
To conclude on the basic warm-up: the pelvis.
Lay your hands on this one like you're superman and circle around (again I know).

The whole thing should barely take a minute, to protect and warm up the joints, it's a given, right?

<u>Performing the advanced joint warm-up:</u>

This warm-up is interesting for the prevention of falls.
We will therefore warm up in addition: wrists, elbows, shoulders and neck.

Wrists: close your fist and turn around your wrist to draw a circle. You can do both at the same time.

Elbows: Place a hand under one of the two elbows and extend the arm with the hand under its elbow. Now, you will bring this same arm towards you, to lower it below the other arm and extend the arm again. A slight natural rotation will occur as you start palm up and end on the other side palm down. Bring the arm back by reversing the movement and repeat the operation at least 10 x per elbow.

Shoulders: Still standing, make sure you're in a room wide enough and high enough not to bump your hand. In order to warm up the shoulder joint draw a circle without bending the arm from back to front. As if you throw a ball for example, except that the circle must be whole and continuous. Once you have done in one direction, do in the other and for the other arm you can repeat the operation.

Neck: Again and again the circles, make a circle very slowly to avoid being dizzy or hurting yourself. Repeat the operation 5x to properly warm up the neck muscles and vertebrae.

Execution of the muscle warm-up:

As mentioned in the name, the high knees consist simply of bringing your knees up alternatively to a 90° angle, all of this whilst having a dynamic stance.

Butt-kicks follow the same process as previously explained, all you need to do is touch your buttocks with your heels as if you were running but by slightly raising your legs higher towards the back. Not everyone can touch their buttocks with their heels, as we don't all have the same morphology, and so some have shorter legs than others. In that case you can just raise your legs as high as possible without pushing too hard on the knees.

To avoid a somewhat repetitive warm-up, you can also do a little jogging or simply a jump rope session, which will allow you to properly finalize your joint and muscle warm-up.

Why warm up?

I know that many of you don't want to warm-up but to get you going here are the main benefits of warming up:

- The risk of injury, whether it be muscular or joint related, will decrease
- Better performance, as your muscles will be warmed up, which can improve the pop (height of the ollie)
- Decrease of cardiovascular risks → I know that you're not old but still!
- And lastly a good warm-up will enable the body to be better prepared, you'll feel a lot readier and more confident.

After your session will come **the stretches.**

You'll mostly ache at the beginning. With training you'll obtain more muscle in your legs and this will considerably reduce the aches. It will all depend on the intensity of the sessions.

Once again it will all depend on the muscle structure of your legs, the more you train your legs with more intense sessions and a good recuperation, the more you'll be protected from aches throughout time.

The stretches after the session

As previously addressed stretches will in a way "relax" the muscles. If you don't stretch after a while you'll feel the consequences in your legs.

Of course, you'll see this for yourself, your pop will be lower as your muscles will feel tired. Your endurance will also decrease which will then shorten your session.

If you give yourself a few minutes before and after each session, your body will thank you and your performances will continue to improve with each session.

There are a total of three muscle groups to stretch: quads, hamstrings and calves.
To stretch the hamstrings (back of the thighs), you just need to bend over and try to touch your toes without bending your knees. Be careful not to hurt your back whilst doing so and

make sure to keep it straight. Maintain this position for 10 to 20 seconds, you should feel the stretch immediately. You can also do this sitting down by touching your toes with your legs stretched out in front of you. For those who can't quite do this just go as far as you can by touching your tibias before reaching your toes.

For the quads, the stretches are done one muscle at a time. Start with the leg of your choice, for example the left one. Stand up, grab your left foot with your left hand and hold it against your buttocks, maintain this position for 10-20 seconds and then do the same with your right leg.

Lastly, for the calves, stand in front of a wall and incline yourself towards it, as if you were going to do a push up, the only difference is that you have to have one leg closer to the wall. Keep the other leg inclined at a 45° angle, it's this leg that you're going to be stretching. After a few seconds you should feel the pull in your calf. You can then do the same with the other leg.

N.B: stretches are done after the session, if not then you'll notice that your performances will slightly decrease and so will your pop!

As I know that it's always better through film, I have made you a little QR code to show you this quicker. There are a lot of exercises done in this video, but you don't have to do as many.

Injuries: prevention and first aid

During your career as a skateboarding world champion, you will surely encounter more than one more or less serious injury. No matter how serious these are, I advise you to treat them as soon as possible. Some injuries can get worse and take over your professional or private life, for example. I myself have known, and you will surely know some of them, who will have to put an end to all sports practice, temporarily or even permanently following a poorly treated injury.

For you and your loved ones, take care of your health, an accident can happen quickly and an injury should not be taken lightly.

<u>Most common injuries in skateboarding:</u>

Wounds: Appears very often following a fall on concrete that is not smooth, it can lead to more or less abundant bleeding depending on its depth and width.

The wound is healed in three stages:

1. Cleaning with lukewarm water
2. Disinfection using a compress and an antiseptic
3. Protect with an adhesive bandage.

Then do as little movement as possible where the wound is.

If it gets worse, gets infected, or doesn't heal, see a doctor.

Hematomas/bruises (or ecchymosis): Hematomas and bruises are rushes of blood under the surface of the skin following a shock. They can be of different sizes and colors depending on the force of the impact and the stage of their evolution.

You will often have them in the tibia, the front part of the leg between the ankle and the knee. In particular because of badly landed 360° tricks or when falling on the side of the body which often leads to bruises on the buttocks, hips and elbows. They are less serious than a wound, tendonitis, or sprain.

The classic solution: Apply ice or a cold source indirectly (ice bag wrapped in a towel, for example) so as not to burn the skin with the cold. There is also arnica which can help and of course leave the body at rest.

Tendinitis: This is an inflammation of a tendon.

Knees, heels, shoulders and wrists are the most affected areas in skateboarding. The area can sometimes be swollen. Tendonitis can occur due to lack of warm-up, extreme conditions (too cold/hot), lack of hydration...

As with bruising, a pocket of cold will calm the pain temporarily. We rest and we avoid movements. _Consult a doctor to confirm the diagnosis and see if there will be a need for rehabilitation._

Sprain: This is the trauma of the ligaments that support a specific joint.

A sprain can be more or less serious and should therefore not be taken lightly. The ligaments can be stretched or ruptured and this can be accompanied by a dislocation or a fracture.

What to do ?: Immediately stop any movement and consult the appropriate medical personnel as soon as possible.

Less common or even rare injuries:

Ligament/tendon/muscle tear, bone fracture, head trauma...

These injuries are the most serious, you should not try to treat yourself but consult the emergency room, a doctor as soon as possible, as well as a physiotherapist for future rehabilitation. Don't take them lightly, I'm watching you.

All this to say that the warm-up is not only for high-level athletes but for all people who practice physical activity. The human body is like a car, if it starts in 5th gear, it will not appreciate and be damaged. Without maintenance, it won't work well in the long term either. You have to prepare it and build a crescendo. It's the same with the body. The ideal is to warm up, hydrate properly during practice (ideally water), take breaks, stretch, take care of yourself and consult the doctor when necessary, and ideally to the ideal... wear protective gear. At least one helmet is the vital minimum. Your body, your brain and your loved ones will thank you.

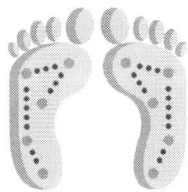

Knowing your stance

Throughout your skating adventure you'll meet two types of skaters:

- the goofy
- the regular

The stance is the position that the skater has on his board, as mentioned above there are only two. It's for you to know which one you'll be, no one will decide for you.

In short, you have two solutions to determine your stance:

1 - If you fall forward, which foot do you put down first?
2 - Get on the board without pushing forward, which foot did you put on first?

Left foot first → Regular
Right foot first → Goofy

As you can guess the regular skater has his left foot at the top of the board and his right foot at the bottom.

It's the opposite for the goofy, he has his right foot at the top of the board and his left at the bottom.

Once this step has been completed, we'll move on to the more serious stuff: riding!

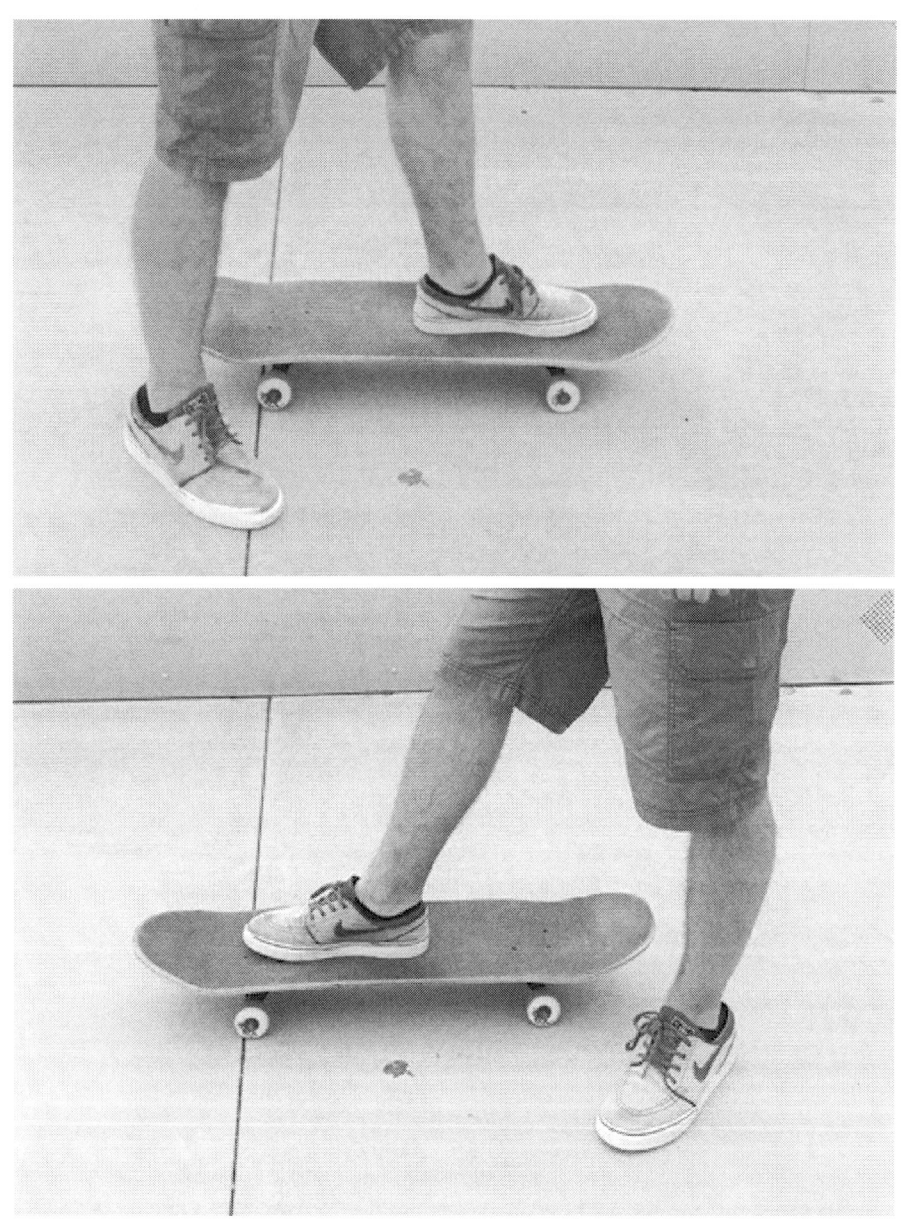

Photos in stationary position in Regular then Goofy stance.

Above, a mad being taking the unconscious risk of pushing Mongo (see the Glossary for more details on this abomination, no I'm kidding, it's like the Mall grab... we talk a lot about it for not much) .

Fakie, nollie, switch? What's this ?

Fakie comes from the contraction of Fake and Nollie. Why ? Simply because the fakie simulates rolling backwards, while simulating being in Nollie for a skater at the opposite stance to yours.
Example: if you are Goofy, in fakie you will be on the Nose of a Regular skateboarder, and vice versa.

And for the Nollie? You have the ollie where you put your back foot on the tail and the other just before the 4 top screws. For the Nollie and all Nollie tricks, we will reverse all foot positioning. There is a dedicated Nollie trick tip on the following pages. If you follow the logic that I have just explained, you will only need to know the positioning of the feet for each of the tricks to then know how to do them in Nollie.

To conclude on a high note: the switch. To put it simply when you are skating in switch, or doing a trick in switch, for example the switch Ollie. You are simply in the other stance: if you are Regular, you will do your Ollie in Goofy, and the reverse for Goofy. As with the Nollie, there is a dedicated Switch Ollie trick tip.

You have understood everything ?

A quick recap:

Nollie: your normal stance, but your front foot will go on the nose (opposite of Ollie)

Fakie: Roll backwards but same foot positioning for all fakie tricks (a fakie ollie is exactly the same as an ollie, just like kickflip etc, EXCEPT you roll backwards, we'll get to that)

Switch: Your opposite stance: the goofy skater becomes Regular. The Regular becomes Goofy.

Know how to ride in skate

At first it's a little difficult and that's normal, it takes time for the brain to learn how to manage the balance correctly. Like when you learn to ride a bike or rollerblade, it's the same thing.

But why?

Simply because you're not used to balancing yourself that way. People that do gymnastics, ice skating or even surfing will have better basics and less difficulty than someone who doesn't do any of those sports.

For an easy start you'll have to determine your stance, as you may have seen on the previous page. And so, you're either a goofy or a regular.

Get on the board and respect your stance.

If you're a goofy → right foot on the top of the board, below the two higher screws.

If you're a regular → left foot on the top of the board, below the two higher screws.

Now put some weight onto that foot and get onto the board. You can now put your other foot on the bottom of the board. There you are, half of the work is done!

To ride, your feet must be in a parallel position in order to better maintain your balance.

To finish up you just need to push down on the ground with your back foot. The push should be light at the start, just enough to move forward while keeping your balance. After the push don't forget to put your feet back in a parallel position to keep your balance.

As you will move forward through your skateboarding experience you will learn to push harder with your legs which will take you further at full speed.

You now know how to ride, make the most of it and do a few descents in order to get used to handling **your balance and the speed.**

Knowing how to turn

To turn, you need to go at a certain pace otherwise it's not very useful.

There are two ways you can turn, for the first way you need to have the trucks a little loose and for the second way there are no prerequisites.

To start with the first way, which is easier, you'll move at a moderate pace, maybe even quickly.

To turn to the left, slightly lean forward to put more weight on your toes which will deflect the board slowly towards the left.

You'll turn more or less quickly but that depends on a few things: the tightness of the kingpin on the trucks, the weight that you put onto the front or back of the board and lastly the speed.

The more your trucks are loose the quicker you can turn and the easier it will be. But it's a choice, each skater has his preferences which has its advantages and disadvantages. It's for you to choose depending on your preferences. The best is to try both!

The second way to turn can be done on the ground as well as on a ramp and at any speed.

Which consists of pushing on the tail, meaning the curved part of the back of the board and swaying your shoulders to the left or to the right.

You will (slightly) turn your hips and shoulders towards the way that you want to turn, without forgetting to gently push on the tail.

Be careful in managing your strength while you push down on the tail, you need to learn the in-between: neither too strong nor too weak. If you push too hard the tail will rub against the ground and it will be difficult to turn. On the other hand, too weak and the wheels will rub against the ground, it will also be just as hard to turn. To succeed you need to find the right balance!

Don't forget that perseverance always pays! No discipline can be learned with the snap of a finger.

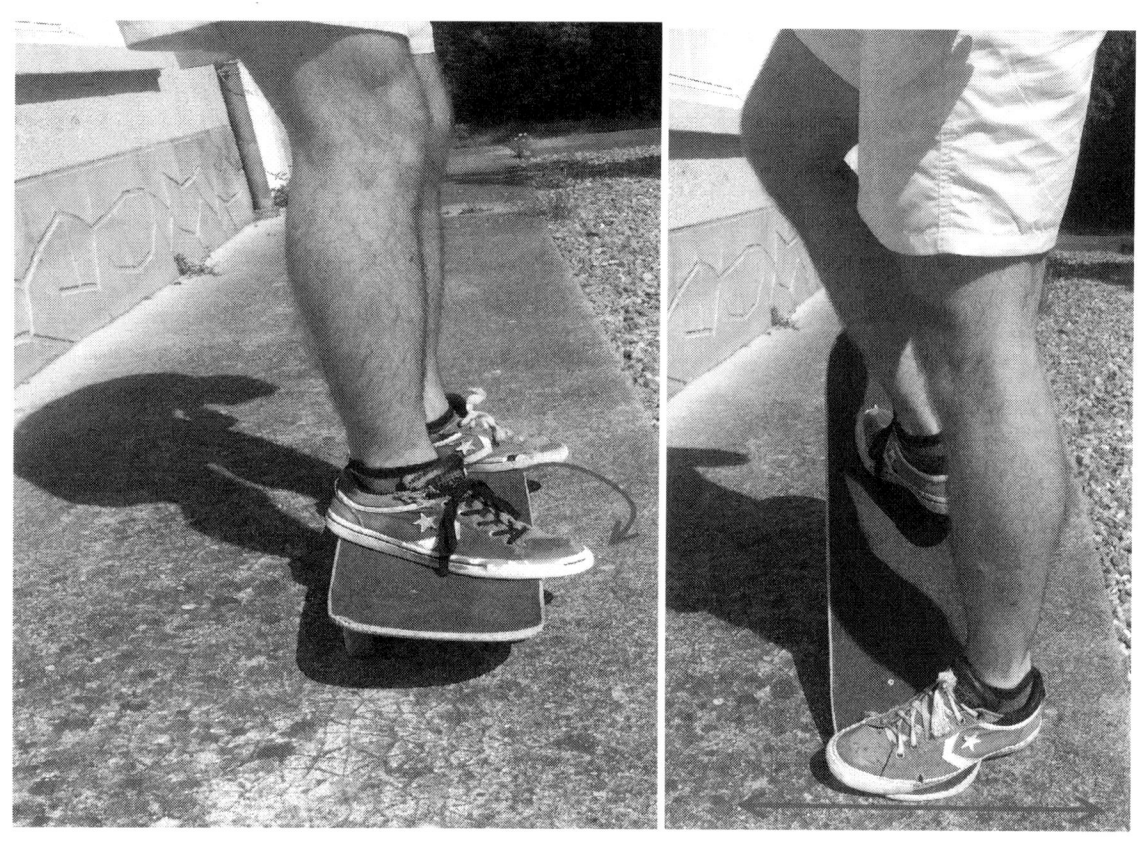

Flat section

      In this first section you will learn the basic tricks for beginners and more advanced skaters. There are only tricks here to do on the ground, you won't need a skatepark or ramps, rail... Only you and your skateboard. However, a soft concrete ground is recommended to maintain your speed.

To start skating off well, I'd advise you, if you haven't already, to read the chapter "Before jumping on your skateboard". I'll remind you that it's better to take on the basic tricks to start off with, so that you don't get frustrated trying to learn the hardflip by jumping off 10 steps.

Of course, you're free to roam between the different sections throughout the book: flat, grind, grab, ramp. In order to discover what to expect as you progress.

A few beautiful and smooth flat tricks :

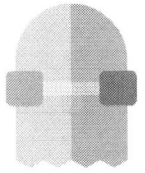

Ollie

Prerequisites: know how to move forward and turn.

The first basic trick to learn is the ollie, which consists of putting pressure on the tail of your board and to scrape the grip with your front foot.

Imagine that it's just a jump on your board and nothing more, this will help you to be on your way. The pressure on the tail as well as the scraping of it just allows the board to stay under your feet.

Just tell yourself that the ollie is a jump.

The ollie is far from simple, it will take more than one try to learn the gesture of the trick without the jump alone.

Once you've acquired the move, you'll start to do tiny jumps of barely 10 cm, then you'll need to jump higher and bend your knees to the max.

That's why I have to remind you that it's just like a jump.

Crouch down, jump and bend your knees to the max.

The trick step by step:

1 – move forward at a moderate pace
2 – place your feet as shown on the following photo

3 – crouch down whilst absorbing the shock of the jump: slam the tail down to the ground with your back foot.
4 – Now scrape the front of the board using the front foot whilst bending your legs to the max
5 – slam down to the ground whilst absorbing the shock with a slight bend of the knees.

A good Ollie: imagine a simple jump, and always pop the tail with force and bend your legs.

And the fakie Ollie?

First of all you have to learn to ride in fakie:
Place your skateboard on the ground with your tail up and your nose down.
Rather than pushing in your normal direction, you have to learn to push in switch. Right foot up for the regular, left up for the goofy. Do the push.
Then to position yourself in fakie, your left foot (right for the regular) will go on the tail.
There, you are driving in fakie!

Then to do your fakie Ollie, everything is the same. With your feet in the same position, get down, slam the tail and land. Everything is the same except that you ride in fakie.

We will come back to this but you can already learn to ride in switch (your opposite stance).

Bonus: Aaron Homoki doing an unimaginable gap

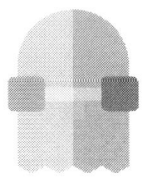

Manual

Prerequisites : know how to ride and turn

A trick that is loved by a lot of skaters.
To make it simple, it's the equivalent to a wheeling. Multiple types of manual exist: two wheels in front, two wheels behind, with the front foot on the nose or even on the tail. It's also possible to add a trick before falling into manual or before doing it. The possibilities are vast, you are free to do what you wish. I'll teach you some more further along in this book.

For the placement of your feet in Manual, there is nothing more simple! Put your back foot on the tail and the front foot on the four screws at the top. Your feet will almost be parallel, I did say almost! The front will be very slightly diagonal, precisely by 17°! Nah just joking.

The trick step by step:

1. Done with the messing around, to start off this trick you need speed so push on your foot as if you want to take over a train.
2. Once you're at the speed of light, place your feet as indicated above or as shown in the photos below
3. Don't joke around with that! Now all you need to do is push down slightly on the tail so that the nose lifts up but without the tail scraping the ground.
4. Everything lies in the management of the balance between the two.

5. Now that you're doing a nice little Manual, and that everyone is looking at you like a demigod you have to push back down, all you need to do is put weight onto the front of the board and you're done!

A little tip from the coach: straightening your arms out helps with your balance and speed.

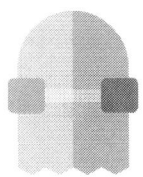

Shove-it

Prerequisites: To do this trick you don't have to know how to do an Ollie, even if with this you'll be able to do a Pop shove-it which is the pop version of the shove-it. That one is definitely nicer.

The shove-it is generally the second trick that all skaters learn after the ollie. It remains in the easy tricks section. Moreover, it opens many doors to new tricks!

The trick step by step:

1. Move at a normal pace
2. Position your feet as shown in the photos below.
3. You'll do a scissor movement, which means that your front foot will balance the board towards your front and the back foot towards your back.
4. The board will do a 180 ° turn, you'll remain above while slightly bending your legs.
5. Cushion the blow, slam down and go off towards new adventures.

For the pop version, all you need to do is slam the tail on the ground while doing the scissor movement. First of all, I would recommend doing the shove-it version and then the pop version: pop shove-it in order to really learn the scissor movement.

The shove-it and its fakie, nollie and switch versions :

The shove-it may be your first experience with the fakie, nollie and switch. If you tire yourself out learning the 4-way shove-it, your fight won't be in vain. This will allow you to expand your range of tricks and open up future trick possibilities. As I previously wrote in the chapter "Fakie, nollie, switch? Kezako?" Every trick to do in another position is nothing special if you master the basic trick.
For the fakie version of the shove-it, you just need to roll in fakie (also described in Fakie, nollie, switch? Kezako?). And to position your feet and do everything like a classic shove-it.

For the Nollie version of the trick, ie Nollie Bs Shove-it, you will have to completely reverse your foot positions. Your front foot will go over your nose, and your back foot will go in the middle of the board or just before the top 4 screws. Finally, do not forget to also reverse the movement of the scissor, that is to say that it is the back foot that will send backwards this time and not the front foot. And yes, everything is reversed in Nollie.
If you nailed the Nollie Shove-it, the Switch shouldn't be a problem. If you are Regular, put yourself in Goofy, and vice versa for Goofy. Position yourself as for the shove-it. Left foot in the middle (or 4 screws from the top) for the Goofy and the same thing but on the right foot for the regular.
The other foot will go on your tail, the movement of the scissor is always the same, we send forward with the foot which is in the middle of the skate.
Now you have mastered the shove-it on its 4 stances! Congratulations ! ;)

Backside and Frontside 180°

Prerequisites: Ollie

Just like the shove-it, the 180° will open many doors for you. And so, it's quite important to learn it, moreover it's the first trick with a physical rotation.

The Frontside 180° step by step:

1. You're on your board at a moderate pace, nor too fast nor too slow.
2. Your feet will be in a parallel position on the board, just like a simple Ollie, the below photo shows the correct way to position your feet.
3. slightly turn your pelvis and shoulders towards your back, very slightly (important for the rest).
4. When you're ready, bend your legs and slam your ollie while continuing the rotation with your pelvis.
5. Once in the air do a rotation towards the back using your pelvis, shoulders and legs.
6. Push the board back down slowly.

If you have correctly done the 180° you should continue in a Fakie and the trick is a success.

In the opposite case your board just stopped and you can't move forward, it's a miss because there isn't enough rotation.

Really think about doing the complete rotation using your body, because it's the rotation that makes the trick a success.

This trick tip is valid for the frontside version as well as the backside version, it's all in the hips and shoulders. For the backside, you've guessed it, you just need to turn your hips and shoulders in the opposite direction.

NB: You can give inertia using your arms when starting the trick.

Positioning of the feet in frontside.

Positioning of the feet in backside.

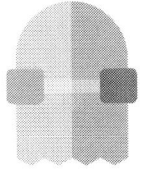

Nollie

Prerequisites: the ollie in order to know the movement.

The nollie is simply the opposite of the ollie. You push down with your front and back foot, the back one will scrape the board to send it towards the stars.

The trick proceedings:

1- Move forward at a moderate pace, nor too slow nor too fast.

2- Place your feet in a parallel position: the front foot on the nose and the other in the middle.

3- crouch down, like doing a classic ollie, in order to reduce the impact on your legs after.

4- Push down on the nose using all your strength, your back foot will scrape the grip towards the tail.

The Nollie gives good sensations when running, once you know how to take it off a few centimeters, try to improve it: roll faster, slam the nose harder and bend your legs as much as possible.

To improve the trick: really think about bending your legs to the maximum and pop the nose with all your strength. The procedure is the same as with Ollie!

Regular	Goofy

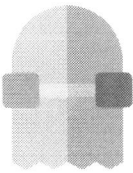

Frontside Shove-it

Prerequisites: the shove-it helps to understand the movement, but it isn't essential.

The frontside shove-it is similar to the shove-it that you previously learnt. The only difference is the order in which you start, for the frontside you'll be throwing yourself backwards instead of forwards, like the classic shove-it.

To know how to place your feet see the photos on the next page.

The trick step by step:

1 - Move forward at a moderate pace
2 - Crouch down and slam the tail down by doing the reverse scissor movement → back foot balanced towards the front and the front foot towards the back.
3 - Jump back to stay above the board by bending your knees
4 – Grab the board, cushion the blow and slam down with your arms in the air!

You would have guessed, it's exactly like the shove-it but with an opposite movement.

Kickflip

Prerequisites: Ollie
It's possible to learn the Heelflip first and then the Kickflip, the order has no importance.

The kickflip is part of the legendary tricks invented by the skater Rodney Mullen. It's one of the most aesthetic and appreciated tricks.

The trick step by step:

1. You're moving at a normal pace, not too slow nor too fast
2. Your back foot is placed the same as for the ollie
3. The front foot placed diagonally between the top two screws
4. Crouch down to prepare for the pop
5. Now everything is like an ollie, the difference being that your front foot will scrape diagonally and not forward
6. Your board will rotate on itself below your legs
7. Once the rotation is done slam down

Really thinking about the ollie will help you because you must be above the board during the entire time. For those who already know the heelflip you'll be a lot less scared of slamming down and so you'll learn it a lot faster. Some skaters find that the heelflip is easier to learn than the kickflip, it's for you to judge and have your own opinion about it. Don't hesitate to slam down half way through the movement to learn the trick, meaning the side where the drawing is.

NB: You'll most likely do a few slicings while you learn the kickflip. This means you'll be landing with both feet on the side of the board (which is barely over 1 cm). This hurts but you get used to it with time, it's the risk that comes with skateboarding.

Don't forget that falling makes it easier to get back up !

Heelflip

Prerequisites: the ollie, the kickflip is optional

For those who already know how to do the kickflip, the heelflip is very much like its twin brother: the kickflip. The difference being that your board will rotate the other way.
For those who still don't know what I'm talking about, and who are learning their first flip-trick, the heelflip is basically your board that will completely turn on itself below your feet within a few milliseconds. You can see the video with the QR code on the next page if you still don't see what a flip-trick is.

The trick step by step:

1. You're moving at a normal pace
2. Your feet are in the same position as for the Fs Pop Shove-it
3. Crouch down
4. Now everything is like an ollie, the difference being that your front foot will scrape diagonally (towards the front)
5. Your board will rotate on itself below your feet in the opposite direction of the kickflip
6. Once the board has done a full rotation, carry your courage and slam down.

Advice for the heelflip:

The mistake that a lot of beginners make is to jump forward and then the board lands behind you. To eliminate this mistake, you really have to think the same way as if you were doing an ollie: keep straight, parallel above the board.

Those who already know the kickflip will learn the heelflip a lot quicker than those who have no flip-tricks on their list of tricks. Never be afraid to fall because of the slicing.

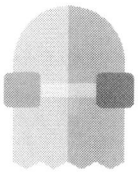

Bs Revert

Prerequisites: None, apart from feeling at ease on the board on flat.

The revert is important to learn. Probably not as essential as the ollie, but nonetheless important to own as it opens many doors.

The trick step by step:

1. Move at a fast pace
2. Your feet positioned as followed:
    1. front > on the 4 top screws slightly in a diagonal position outwards
    2. back > on the tail, the tip of the toe towards the top
3. First of all, you're going to turn your shoulders inwards (backside) which will make your hips and then legs follow. Push down on these in order to make the wheels slip on the ground until you do a complete 180° turn.
4. To do that your legs need to do the scissors: the back leg has to push towards the back and the front one towards the front.
5. If all is ok, you should be on your way in switch.

Don't hesitate to spread your legs, the front foot has to really be far apart, it shouldn't touch the nose. Really think about putting a lot of force into your legs to do the scissors effect.

The +: Once acquired you'll be able to learn it in frontside, and in 360° but for this one you'll need a much smoother surface. It's also possible to do it on wet ground, try your luck.

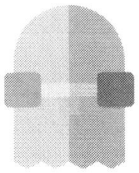

Nose Manual

Prerequisites: mastering the manual at first will be a good basis to learn the management of the balance in nose manual. This is not mandatory but will strongly help you to learn the nose manual which is more difficult to manage than the manual.

The positioning of the feet is always as usual, we let his small eyes admire the photos below depending on your stance. Nothing complicated to report since it is exactly the opposite of the manual: front foot on the nose, rear foot at the screws.

Steps of the trick:

1. Roll fast enough.

2. Position your feet as in the photo corresponding to your stance.

3. Press the nose lightly and add weight to the back foot.

4. Manage the balance between the two, the nose should not rub and the rear wheels should not touch the ground.

5. Once you are satisfied with your length, replicate and ride to new adventures.

N.B: As with the manual, stretching out your arms on the sides will help you manage the balance. I also specify (although I'm sure you can imagine), that it will be easier to learn on the ground, so do not bother to start on a piece of pavement or other "manual pad".

Goofy	Regular

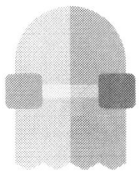

360° Shove-it

Prerequisites: The ollie and the pop shove-it, the non-pop version will also work.

The 360° shove-it in skateboarding is a trick that requires a good level to start it off. If not, then this trick will cause a lot of slicing. This fault happens often to skateboarders who know the kickflip or the 360° flip because they are used to starting the flip with the front foot. Which very often ends in slicing! But of course, it is possible to do both.

The trick step by step:

1. Move at a moderate pace
2. Your feet are positioned like the following photo
3. Everything is done the same as for a classic shove-it but with more power
4. Your feet will give as much power as possible
5. Jump as high as you can while following the board below your feet.
6. slam down and cushion the blow

Try to avoid scraping your front foot when starting off the trick in order to avoid making the board flip.

There are two ways to do the trick:
1- The pop version: it's more difficult but neater, with a bigger risk of slicing
2- The low version: More simplified, less neat, less risk of slicing

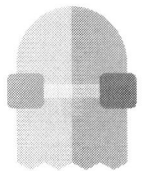

Disco Shove-it / Shove-it sex change

Prerequisites: The Pop Shove-it, as well as the body varial (jump 180° while rolling without touching the board) can help you.

If you've ever dabbled in old school tricks later in the book, you've no doubt seen disco kickflip, which involves performing a kickflip by rotating the body 180°. Here we will repeat the operation but with a shove-it.
As usual, the fakie version is easier to make, so feel free to start with this one.

To know that the tricks in disco are always done in the opposite direction of the rotation of the board. Here we are doing a backside shove-it, not a frontside. It is therefore you who turn on the frontside side to land on the skate.
At first, do not hesitate to practice by sending the board and turning without landing on it.

Procedure of the trick:
1. Ride at a moderate pace, feet positioned as for a classic shove-it/pop.
2. Launch the shove-it with the feet while sending pelvis and shoulders in the opposite direction (frontside).
3. Jump up, bending your legs slightly while continuing the rotation.
4. Land softly while cushioning.
5. Cheer !

That's it, not complicated, is it? Do not hesitate to add a little revert once you are comfortable. Like all the other tricks, this one too can be combined with other tricks. In fact, you can do everything with a body variant, from Ollie to 360 flip to hardflip etc. Give free rein to your imagination and have fun trying the variants that appeal to you the most!

A game of skate with only body varial :

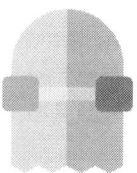

Varial flip

Prerequisites: the pop shove-it and the kickflip are essential

The varial kickflip is a highly appreciated trick by skateboarding amateurs.
This one is easier to learn and, for some, easier than the kickflip. The varial kickflip is a fusion between the pop shove-it and the kickflip. All you need to do is to imagine a shove-it mixed with a kickflip, both tricks at the same time of course.
And it's as easy as that.

The trick step by step:

1. Move at a normal pace, nor too fast nor too slow.
2. Position your feet as shown on the following photos.
3. Prepare the bob by crouching down.
4. Go back up all whilst slamming the tail of your board.
5. Your back foot will start the shove-it and the front one the kickflip with less power to scrape the flip.
6. The board flips and turns into a shove-it at the same time.
7. Once both rotations are done: slam down slowly.

During the 4 stage, really think about the pop, the higher the trick is done above ground the more time you'll have to grab the board and avoid slicing. It's a valuable piece of advice for any trick that has a flip in it.

If you do slicing (board that lands on the side): give more impulses into your front foot, the one that starts the flip off.

If the board doesn't do a 180° turn: slam your back foot harder to intensify the movement of the rotation in the shove-it.

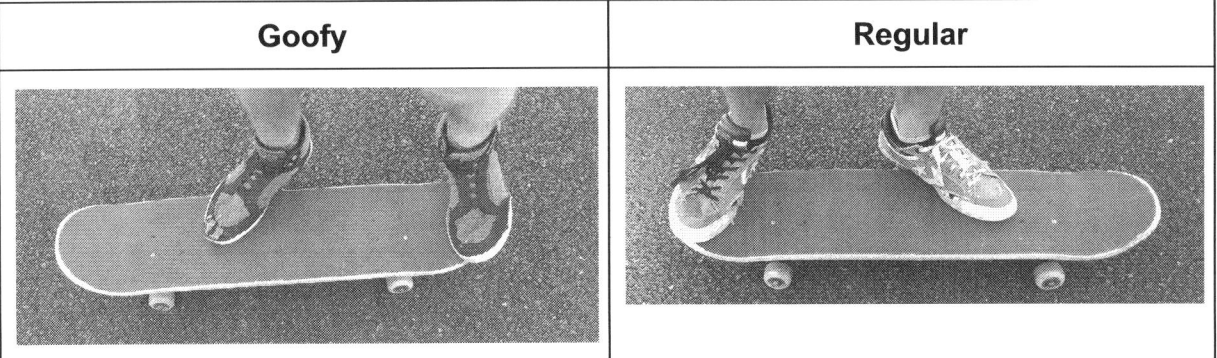

Goofy	Regular

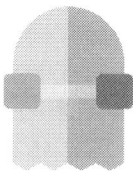

Fakie Bs Bigspin

Prerequisites:

- shove-it and/or Fakie shove-it
- Backside 180° and/or Fakie backside 180°
- Optional: The fakie 360° shove-it

The Fakie Big spin is a really simple trick to obtain and very nice to give someone a letter in the skating game. It's generally the first big spin that we learn because it's more accessible.

A fakie big spin is a big spin but in fakie. Until now nothing too hard.
A big spin is the pure combination of a 360° shove-it and a 180° rotation of the body (here in backside 180°)

The trick step by step:

1. To start off, you're moving at a normal pace (not too slowly) in fakie.
2. Position your feet exactly the same as for the shove-it.
3. For now you're riding in fakie, just chilling on your board
4. You'll start your shove-it at the same time that your body starts the rotation.
5. Normally, your board will start it's rotation, and then your body
6. To practice, you can slam the fakie big spin down halfway, meaning your body will have only done half of the rotation,

same thing for your board, a shove-it as well as 90° of the rotation.

Don't forget: I'll remind you that speed really helps for this trick, because it helps the board to do a rotation. The Fakie Big spin is a fusion between the Fakie bs 180° and the Fakie 360° Shove-it. And so it's more important to concentrate on the rotation in order to guarantee the completion of the trick.

Don't hesitate to get started quicker whilst imagining a Fakie Backside 180°!

Goofy	Regular

Nollie Bs 180

Prerequisites: the nollie is mandatory as you can imagine, which is completely normal!
To that I'll add the frontside 180°.

First of all let me just add something important for the rest of the trick. As we've seen before, the Backside 180° in normal position is doing a rotation towards the inside, which is the opposite to the frontside where halfway through we are seen facing sideways, it's in the name "front". Same goes for the back where halfway through we are seen facing backwards.

Whereas with the nollie the rules are opposite. For a matter of fact the same goes for the grinds and slides. I didn't make this rule up. I'm just applying it so that you know it and that you don't make any mistakes.

So as you would have understood, here the Nollie 180° will not be towards the inside but towards the outside. Just like a classic frontside 180 ° but in Nollie, of course.

The trick step by step:

1. Move at a moderate pace
2. Your feet are positioned like in the following photos, depending on your stance. You can't change a winning team.
3. Now everything is done the same way as for a frontside 180°, first slightly place your shoulders like a frontside and then slam the nollie.

4. Once you've slammed, slightly bend your legs and finish the 180° rotation whilst always using your shoulders and pelvis.
5. slam down softly, cushion the blow and continue in fakie.
6. Bow down and wave to your public for that magnificent performance.

N.B: The position of your feet is very important here, as you can see your front foot will be in the top corner on the right of the nose which will make the rotation easier in frontside, just as the back foot, slightly over the back of the board, will do the same job.

Goofy	Regular

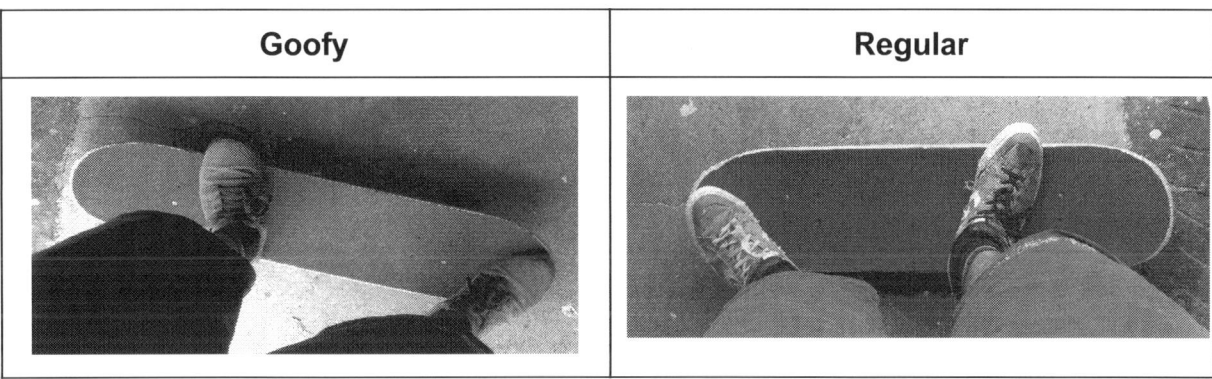

Nollie Bs Pop Shove-it

Prerequisites: It's preferable to know the nollie as well as the Fs pop shove it in normal position.

It's a very cool trick to learn, as a matter of fact it's one of my favorites.
Once you know it on a flat surface I would recommend you learning it on a more inclined surface, sensations guaranteed!
Moreover it's not really that complicated to learn, it's even easier if you already know both prerequisites previously listed.

The trick step by step:

1. You're moving at a moderate pace, not as slow as an old man though
2. Your feet are in the same position as for a nollie Bs 180 °, as seen before but with the front foot slightly higher.
3. Crouch down and slam the nollie
4. Normally, just with the position of your feet the shove-it should launch naturally. If that's not the case then don't hesitate to accompany the board a bit like for the Fs Shove-it as previously seen.
5. The board will do its rotation, stay above it, and then land on the board softly.
6. Congratulations!

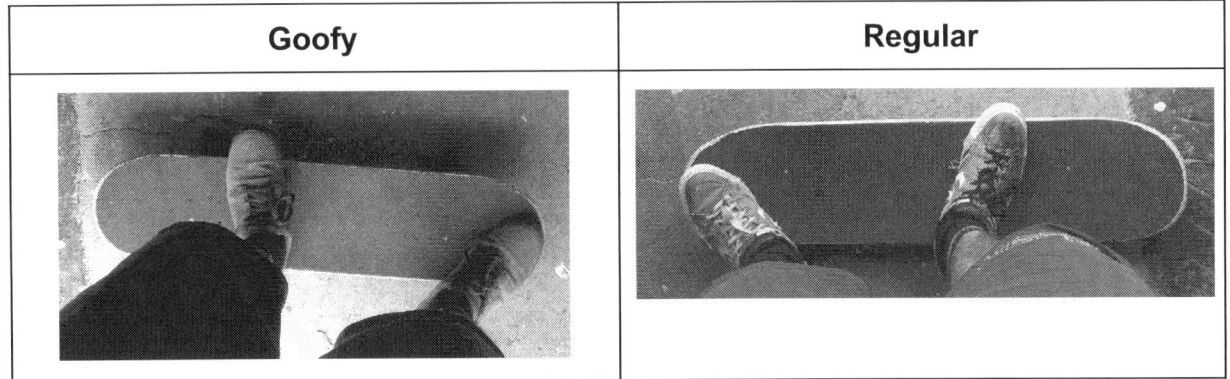

Nollie Bs Bigspin

Prerequisites: The Nollie Bs 180° and the Nollie Bs pop shove-it are mandatory, young rascal.

If you have carefully learnt both of the previous trick tips then you should be able to learn this trick correctly. The difficulty level is a little higher, however it's still a quite easy and practical trick.
All it is, is the fusion between a nollie Bs 180° and a 360° shove-it, in the same position. Hold on tight and let's be off!

The trick step by step:

1. your feet are positioned the same as for a nollie Bs Shove-it, as previously seen.
2. The same as for a flip with rotation, you have to be 100 % concentrated on the rotation and not on the trick itself, you should be able to launch the trick without even thinking about it.
3. As soon as you launch it you'll need to send your shoulders and pelvis forward before slamming the nollie.
4. Slam the nollie and accompany the board in its 360° rotation shove-it with the help of your feet.
5. Continue the physical rotation all whilst letting the board finish its 360 ° rotation.
6. slam down in fakie/switch
7. And here you are happy!

A tip from the coach: Before entirely learning the trick (360 ° rotation of the board and 180° rotation of the body), split it in half and simply do a 90° rotation with the body and a shove-it with an extra 90° rotation on the board. This will make you stop suddenly, but this technique will help you learn the trick a lot faster.

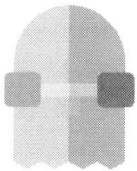

Bs Bigspin

Prerequisites: the 360° shove-it and the Backside 180°

Optional: the fakie big spin, even though it will help you a lot with the trick, it's optional for those who haven't learnt it.

You have previously learnt the fakie version of the big spin. Once the fakie version is acquired, the classic version will be a lot more accessible.

The big spin is a trick that is highly appreciated by skaters for its beauty, and I would even say that it's more aesthetic than the fakie version. Unfortunately this one is more difficult. The slicing can happen more often mainly because the board does a 360° flip in most cases. Or even because of the lack of rotation whether it be from the body or the board.

But don't give up! This trick really deserves to be learnt, not just for the challenge but also for the sensation you get when executing it, which is fabulous whether it be for the skater or the person who is watching.

The trick step by step:

1. Move at a moderate pace

2. Your feet are positioned in the same way as for a 360° shove-it

3. Crouch down and slam down at the tail

4. Your back foot will push down as hard as possible

5. At the same time that you launch the 360° shove-it start your BS 180°.

6. Once the board has done the 360° rotation and you're above it, slam down gently.

If you're missing a few degrees before slamming down 2 solutions are available to you:

The first one is to finish the trick with a little revert. This solution is the easiest one, but your trick will be sketchy.
The second one is to pop your 360° shove-it even more and to jump higher. This one is the best solution out of the two but the hardest.
Once acquired, your trick will be perfect.

NB: As for the Bs 360° shove-it the procedure is the same if you wish to do it in frontside. The placement of your feet is the same as for the Fs Shove-it.

360° Flip

Prerequisites: 360° shove-it, kickflip. The varial kickflip is the one that will help you the most.

The 360 ° flip is probably one of the most mythical tricks in the skating world. That's why it's important to count it in your list of tricks (or not, it's up to you).
Moreover, once you know the move, it's really quite easy to slam down again!
However this is not the easiest trick to learn, say hello to face plants.

Trick proceedings:

1. You're moving at a regular pace, which you'll keep throughout the trick.
2. Your feet are at a 360° angle just like the shove-it (see the next photo)
3. Crouch down to prepare your pop
4. Now everything is going to be like the 360° shove-it, the difference being you'll scrape the flip with your front foot.
5. Imagine a pair of scissors: that's what your legs will do, the back foot backwards and the front foot forwards.
6. slam down the front of the board forward and do a 360° rotation accompanied by a flip.
7. Right after jumping you'll still be in the air above your board
8. Once the 360° rotation and the flip done, slam down softly
9. Congratulations!

Do not forget: this trick is difficult so push through and don't ever give up!!

A bit of advice: the trick is a lot easier to learn in Fakie, so don't hesitate to start with that.

| Goofy | Regular |

Halfcab Heelflip

Prerequisites: - the heelflip and/or fakie heelflip
- the half cab (fakie bs 180°)

A half cab is a 180° backside but in fakie.
So yes, as you just understood the half cab heelflip is a fakie backside 180° heelflip.
And that's it!

But don't back down, it's not as complicated as it seems, on the contrary. And just like the 360° flip, once acquired it's a trick that you'll keep for a long time.

The trick step by step:

1- position yourself in a fakie and move forward at a normal pace.
2- Your back and front foot are positioned exactly the same as for a heelflip
3- Once ready, bend your knees and slam down
4- Do the 180° backside rotation with your hips whilst flipping the board.
5- Your life flashes before your eyes as your board rotates below your feet
6- slam down by flexing your legs and once it's done go get congratulated by your friends.

A little piece of advice:

It's possible that you may do a few side falls (fall on the side of the board) that means that you're putting too much pressure into the flip or not enough.
If you don't do the 180° with your body then think about doing the fakie Bs 180°. Training to do the half cab will be useful to you.

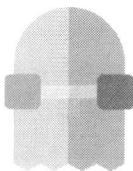

Backside Kickflip / Backside Heelflip

Prerequisites:
Backside 180° -> obligatory!
Kickflip to do the backside kickflip and heelflip for the backside heelflip.

Backside flips are very aesthetic and pleasant to do. Moreover if you can do the prerequisites they won't be too complicated to learn with practice.

As indicated in the name, it's about doing a backside so an ollie backside 180°, as we saw previously, and at the same time a flip. Here you are free to do it as a kickflip or heelflip, I'm regrouping both so that you don't have to read the same thing twice.

To do this trick you really need to concentrate more on the 180° rotation than on the actual flip. You simply need to imagine that you're doing a 180°.

The trick step by step:

1- Move at a normal pace
2- Place your feet depending on the flip you want: kickflip or heelflip
3- Send your shoulders and hips into backside and then slam down the ollie
4- With the front foot, flip the board
5- Continue the 180 ° backside rotation over the board, that is still flipping and turning in back

6- once the 180° done slam down gently and go back into a fakie

Backside Kickflip :

Backside Heelflip :

Backside Heelflip :

Backside Kickflip :

Just like almost all tricks in skateboarding, these tricks are easier to learn in fakie. Why ? Here we have a 180° rotation, so you will land in your normal stance and not fakie if you land in your normal stance. And it will give you an extra trick ;)
Once you have mastered the trick, you have several options:
- Bs double flip/heelflip (a specialty of the famous French skateboarder Bastien Salabanzi)
- Nollie Bs Flip/Heelflip
- Switch Bs Flip/Heelflip
- Cabalerial Flip/Heel (cab = 360° so full body rotation with a flip)
- Backside 360° flip/heel, like a 180° except you will do a full turn.

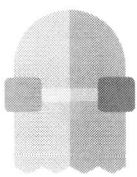

Frontside Kickflip / Frontside Heelflip

Prerequisites: The frontside 180° is mandatory.

If you start the frontside kickflip you'll also need to master the kickflip, same goes for the frontside heelflip where you'll need to master the heelflip.

Personally I think that frontside flips are more difficult to learn than those that we have learnt previously in backside. This is only my opinion, but it's up to you to make your own opinion by trying one or the other depending on which you prefer, as visually they are not at all the same. As for most skateboarding tricks that are done on flat, if you are having trouble you can try to learn them in fakie first.

Indeed, the simple fact of doing the trick in fakie helps a lot of skaters when it comes to slamming, so don't hesitate if this is the case!

The trick step by step:

1. You're moving at a good pace
2. Your feet are in the same position as the targeted flip: kickflip or heelflip
3. open up your shoulders frontside and let your pelvis follow the movement
4. immediately slam the tail the same as for a frontside 180°

5. Start the kickflip, or heelflip, using your front foot all whilst continuing the rotation
6. Finish your rotation in the air while correctly bending your knees
7. Gently slam down and ride off being proud of having succeeded.

As it's the case for the other tricks that have a rotation, you always have to start by concentrating on the rotation itself rather than the trick that comes with it. Maybe even ignoring the trick, because the hardest part is the rotation. Launching the trick at the same time must be secondary in order to succeed.

Frontside Kickflip:

Frontside Heelflip:

Frontside Heelflip:

Frontside Kickflip:

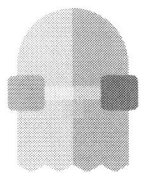

Inward Heelflip

Prerequisites: the heelflip and pop shove-it are mandatory

The inward heelflip, as well as the hard flip, are part of the hardest tricks to learn.
They are in fact the perfect fusion between a pop shove-it and a heelflip.

The trick step by step :

1. Move at a moderate pace
2. Your feet are in the same position as for a heelflip
3. Crouch down to prepare for the trick
4. Stand back up straight and slam at the same time
5. your back foot will give the pressure to go towards the back, the same as for the shove-it
6. Launch the heelflip with your front foot
7. Your board will spin and do it's 180 ° accompanied by the heelflip
8. Once the rotation is complete, slam down

NB: The inward heelflip is a lot easier to learn in fakie than in the normal way.
Don't hesitate to learn the trick little by little: a complete shove-it with a half heelflip. This will allow you to learn to slam down again which is the hardest part.

Goofy	Regular

Varial Heelflip

Prerequisites: Fs Pop shove-it and heelflip

The varial heelflip is a very nice trick and yet it's not used as much as other tricks.
That's why it's important to know it if you want to stand out amongst others and also be the master of the skating game.

The trick step by step:

1. Move at a normal pace
2. Your feet are in the same position as for a Fs pop shove-it
3. Everything is done the exact same way as for a Fs Shove-it
4. Except from the fact that you'll be launching a heelflip with your front foot, this one will do an opposite gesture from the Fs Shove-it which, in this case, will push the board backwards. Here, the front foot will be pushed towards the front in order to launch the heelflip
5. Launch the heelflip and shove-it at the same time
6. Jump back, bend your legs and slam down whilst cushioning the blow

This trick is quite simple if you already know the Fs Shove-it and the heelflip.
If you slam down on the image (bottom side of the board) and/or side of the board (slicing): put more pressure into your heelflip with your front foot.
If you slam down with a non-complete Fs Shove-it: Pop harder backwards and bend your legs.

Tip: Always imagine that you're launching a Fs Shove-it in order to push yourself into jumping backwards.

Goofy	Regular

Hardflip

Prerequisites: the Fs pop shove-it and the kickflip

In skateboarding, the hardflip is one of the hardest tricks. You would have guessed it but that's why the name starts with "hard". Before succeeding for the first time you need, for most skaters, many hours of practice, slicing and a lot of courage.

There is even an urban legend that exists that is shared amongst skaters about this trick: to hit your nose between your crotch.
It's both true and false
Because it all comes down to your footwork, if you jump high or not.
But also in the way you slam it and launch it.

Indeed, there are two methods to launch the trick:

- The first, which is the least dangerous one for your private parts, is to launch it without popping it too much and by jumping as high as possible.
- By doing it this way your trick will be slammed but less neatly than the hardflip in the second method as mentioned below.
- The second, which is a lot more dangerous for your private parts, is to pop with all your strength and by jumping as high as possible.

This method is the most widespread, if you can do it then your hardflip will be perfect.

The visual effect is very different between the two methods, the second method gives a more "raised" effect, that's why it's a lot more dangerous but a lot nicer! By "raised" effect I mean the board will be standing upwards as if you were holding it by the nose. So, if the board goes high enough, thanks to your pop, but that you slam down too quickly, then it's the nutcracker.

The trick step by step:

1. Move at a normal pace
2. Place your feet as shown on the photo below
3. Bend down to prepare for the trick
4. Slam with all your strength, the back foot does a Fs Shove-it and the front one a Kickflip
5. Bend your legs as much as possible
6. The board passes between your legs, wait till the end of the flip and slam down

This trick is difficult so don't give up and persevere until you manage to slam the board.

A little tip: Try it in fakie, it will be a lot easier for those who are starting off. You need to think about not flipping too much with your front foot because the back foot will already make it easy enough.

Goofy	Regular

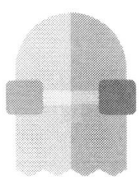

Bigspin Kickflip

Prerequisites: At least the Backside big spin and the backside 180° with ease and also the kickflip.
The 360° flip is a bonus that would REALLY help you.

Some find that the Big spin flip is easier than the 360° flip, for others it's the other way around, so you just might be lucky if you end up in the second group.
Generally, those who are comfortable with 180° rotations are also comfortable with everything to do with the big spin.

Let me start by warning you, this trick is not simple.
But if you've made it this far then it means that nothing much scares you anymore.
So go ahead and change the game!

The trick step by step:

1. Move at a moderate pace, not at 100 mph and not as slow as a granny
2. Your feet are positioned the exact same as for a 360° flip (look at the photos if you don't know dummy)
3. The thing that changes from the 360° flip is the rotation, so before popping start by slightly turning your pelvis and shoulders.
4. Slam the tail as if you were launching a 360° flip.
5. Turn your body as for a backside 180°, really bend your legs
6. Once the 360° flip of the board done, grab the board, slam down and cushion the blow
7. YEEEHAAAAAA

NB: Be careful with the slicing, and don't despair, it's by skating that you become a skater!

In regard to the launch of the 180° and 360° flip your movement must be synchronized to perfection. Because the 180° (shoulders – pelvis) is to be launched first, a few milliseconds before the 360° flip. It's that first 180° rotation that will enable you to basically ignore the fact that you are launching it, and then you'll be able to fully concentrate on the 360° flip.

Goofy	Regular

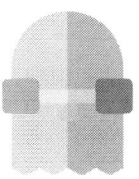

Lazer Flip

Prerequisites: The fs 360° shove-it, the heelflip and the varial heelflip

This trick is quite rare, most skaters choose the kickflip side with the tre flip (360° flip). However, its visual effect is really impressive.

If you want to show who's boss, then you already know what you have to do.

The trick step by step:

1. Move at a normal pace
2. Place your feet in the same position as seen on the photo below
3. Crouch and slam down whilst doing the scissor movement of the 360° shove-it but...
4. The front foot will slightly launch a heelflip because all of the power goes into the back foot
5. The back foot will launch a powerful blow towards the front to launch the Fs 360° shove-it
6. Bend your legs whilst jumping backwards, catch the board and slam down whilst cushioning the blow

It's one of the hardest tricks in the flat so train yourself tirelessly!

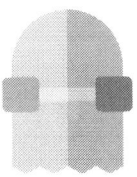

Bigspin Heelflip

Prerequisites: The laser flip and the frontside 180°

As we saw the Big spin kickflip before, it would be impossible not to talk about the heelflip version. The difficulty level is the same, this one is done in frontside and not backside, like for the kickflip version.
Before starting the trick, you need to really master both prerequisites previously mentioned.

The trick step by step:

1. Move at a good pace
2. Your feet are positioned the same as shown on the photos below.
3. Open up your shoulders and pelvis towards the frontside
4. Launch the laser flip with force, all whilst bending your legs in the air
5. Let the board finish it's rotation whilst staying above
6. Slam softly and hope that you avoid the deadly slicing
7. Bravo bravo!!

It's one of the more complicated tricks, so don't neglect the prerequisites before starting it otherwise it will be a long task. A lot of practice will bear its fruit, don't forget that hard work always pays off.

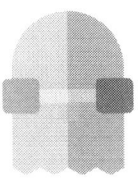

Switch Ollie

Prerequisites: The Ollie
Optional: The Nollie helps a lot

The Switch Ollie is a highly appreciated trick for two reasons. Firstly, as you learn it, you'll be reminded of your beginnings in skateboarding and secondly, which will make you very happy:

- A multitude of new tricks

Why will it remind you of your beginnings?

Simply because you'll feel like you're starting over from scratch, you'll be learning the Ollie again.
This time it will be in switch, meaning in the reverse position.
If you don't know what the switch is in skateboarding it's simply the reverse position. Are you Goofy? You'll become Regular in switch and vice versa for the Regular.

Why will it give you the possibility to learn even more new tricks?

If you hadn't figured it out already, you'll be able to do all of your tricks already learnt, for example the kickflip but in switch. Which will make you learn everything over again, it's a real challenge to impose on yourself but you'll gain more experience and have more tricks to do.

To avoid all complications the tip for this trick will be in two parts, the first one will be for the goofy and the second for the regular.
You know what you have left to do.

Switch Ollie for goofy

The trick step by step:

1. To start off, place yourself in switch position and give a few kicks to gain a bit of speed.
2. You're in switch, place your right foot on the tail and the left one in the center
3. Your feet are parallel, everything is the same as for an Ollie in your normal position
4. Now I'm not going to spell it out for you but you already know the rest (or not but I wouldn't be pleased if that's the case at this point)
5. Slam the tail with your right foot and scrape the ground towards the front of the board to scale it up with the left foot.
6. Bend those legs and slam down gently
7. The doors to the switch are now open to you, enough to put loads of letters in the skating game.

Switch Ollie for Regular

The trick step by step:

1. To start off with, place yourself in switch and then give a few kicks to gain a bit of speed.
2. You're in switch, place your left foot on the tail and the right one in the center
3. Your feet are parallel, everything is the same as for an Ollie in your normal position
4. And now I'm not going to draw it out for you, you already know the rest (or not)
5. Slam the tail with your right foot and scrape the top of the board to give momentum with the left
6. Bend those legs and slam down softly
7. The doors towards the switch are now open to you, enough to give a load of letters to your friends in a game of skate.

Goofy	Regular

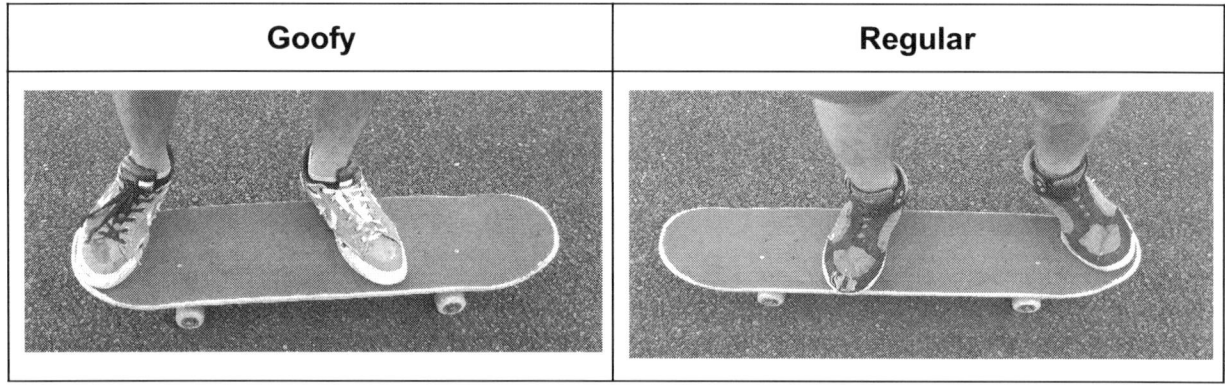

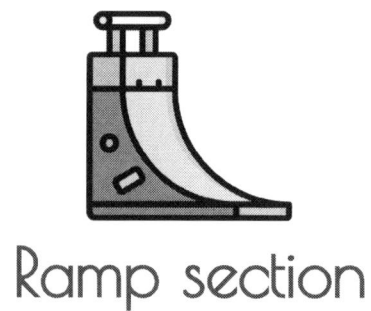

Ramp section

The ramp is the opening of new sensations in skateboarding that you won't feel in flat.

The airs, the stall tricks, curve grinds, grabs and even just the sensation of climbing up and down a curve are things that you can't miss!

Obviously if you don't have a skatepark nearby then it will be a bit difficult, however for those who do have one in your town then don't hesitate for a second in going there!

It's also the occasion to meet other skaters who'll most likely become your future friends!

What you also need to know Is that the ramp is like the flat, it has its risks. So don't start by trying to go down the big ramp if you can't even go down in flat that's inclined by 1 meter. Learn to move forward little by little, slowly but surely. The first basic trick to learn, and is truly indispensable in skateboarding, is the drop but I would advise you to be really comfy before trying the drop.

To be comfy I would advise two easy and quick things to learn:

1. Pumping on a curve
2. Doing a kick turn on a curve

1- Pumping on a curve, this isn't taking your bike pump to pump the wheels of your board on a curve. It's a "trick" that will enable you to easily gain speed on a curve. It's very useful to do tricks in Fakie on a curve, pyramid or simply to obtain a lot more speed in a bowl to go off easily.

How do you do it?

You're arriving face to face with the curve with more or less speed.

You mount the ramp, without the front truck blocking on the curve, because that's not what we're after here. Entirely mount without blocking, the higher you'll go the more speed you'll gain.

Now that you pretty much know how far to go, all that's left to do is to correctly do the gesture. The gesture is simple, but the better you do it the more speed you'll gain. To do so all you need is to crouch down as if you were slamming an Ollie, exactly at the same height but without slamming it. And then to stand back up straight away. The entire movement must be synchronized perfectly with the mounting onto the ramp. Meaning that at the bottom of the ramp you're standing up straight and by the end you're crouched down to the max. It's for you to learn the movement depending on the height of the ramp. The movement requires training before being able to do it perfectly and to gain a consequent amount of speed.

2- Kick turn on the ramp

I'm not going to go back into detail regarding this trick because I've previously detailed it enough in the ground version. If you don't remember it, it's the method in which you turn on the ground by pressing down on the tail.

However you have to know that with the ramp you have to give a lot less pressure on the tail in order to turn. Because otherwise it's a tragedy, and you'll go off in Manual! And on a curve that's nearly inclined to 90° you can quickly imagine what damage it can cause.

And so it's up to you to judge the pressure that you'll put on the tail but it really needs to be less than when turning on the ground because being on the curve will help you turn.

Of course as well as for the version on the ground, you have to use your shoulders and pelvis to help accompany the turn and gain balance.

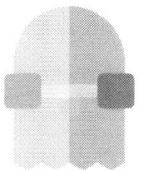

Drop In

Prerequisites: Just be comfy on the ramp, in particular know how to pump on a curve and be able to do kick turns on it.

The very first trick to learn if you want to skate on a ramp. It consists of going down the ramp that's curved and not inclined.
To start off I would advise you to find a small ramp, not one that's higher than your head of course! Unless you don't have a choice.

There you have it, once you have found your ramp, mount it. I'm not going to explain to you how to do it huh?

There you are at the top and now follow these instructions to the letter:

The trick step by step:

1. You're at the top of a curve, the tail pressed on the coping of the ramp. Meaning the tail is against the flat part of the ramp, the back truck and back wheels are pressed against the top of the curve.
2. Your back foot on the tail
3. put the front foot diagonally on the top four screws, without doing anything more.
4. Slightly lean towards the front of the ramp by simply bending the knee of the leg that is at the front of the board
5. Slam with all your strength with your front foot on the ramp by slightly bending your legs.

6. Maintain the balance until reaching the bottom

Advice from the coach: the main difficulty of the drop is the fear of throwing yourself forward towards the ramp. But you'll have to get over this fear in order to pass this step. For those who are a bit more of a scaredy cat, ask your friends to hold both of your hands during the drop. It helps to get started of course. But before anything the best thing is to dare to do it. Protections can also help you with this.
If you haven't understood the movement then don't hesitate to flash the QR code in order to see the video.

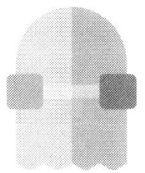

Rock Fakie

Prerequisites: Be comfy on curves, and knowing how to pump is a big advantage.

Another basic trick on the ramp. To do this trick you have to block the front truck onto the coping of the ramp and then go off in Fakie.

For this you need quite a lot of speed, so the best thing is to go down another ramp, which is inclined for example or another curve now that you're a pro when doing the drop!

The trick step by step:

1. Once you've gone down with a sufficient amount of speed go towards a ramp, mount it but not completely, only up to where you can block the front truck of your board.
2. After the truck is correctly positioned, put a bit of weight onto the front of the board in order to maintain the truck blocked for about a second
3. To go off all you need to do is to very lightly press down on the tail all whilst maintaining the balance on the board and leaning slightly backwards
4. Go off in fakie towards new adventures

The + from the coach:

Once you've done it you can push it a bit further and do it like Tony Hawk.
Which means not only blocking the truck but half of the board!
You'll mount the ramp and hit half of your board on the coping aaand then go back down.
And then you'll ask yourself "YEES but coach won't we block the front truck???"
Yes and no, because actually everything is done the same as for the Rock Fakie that you have done before, but you have to slightly press on the tail. I did say slightly, be careful amigo.

Rock n' Roll

Prerequisites: The Rock Fakie will really help you but it's not completely indispensable.

I would advise that you learn this trick just after the Rock Fakie, because you can learn Rock n' Roll quickly if you already know the Rock Fakie. The position of the feet is the same, except from the front foot that is slightly in a diagonal position to help with the rotation.

What? A rotation?

Yes, it's very simple. The Rock n' Roll is actually a Rock assembled with a kick turn. Meaning once the truck is blocked you'll do a kick turn and then go off in the correct direction and not in Fakie like for the Rock.

The trick step by step:

- The Rock n' Roll starts the same as the Rock but once the truck is blocked you need to make a 180° rotation on the back wheels. All you need to do is to put more weight onto the back wheels when you go off and it's done!

The tip:

Mainly, don't hesitate to place your body in a parallel position on the board, you'll gain time and the rotation will be done much faster.
The same as for the Rock Fakie, this trick can be done more neatly by blocking the middle of the board, guaranteed effect!

The main difficulty of this trick resides in the rotation, because mounting the ramp alone is already hard enough so let alone doing a rotation on top of that!
You really need to use your pelvis, shoulders and arms to help you do the rotation in the backside. The same as for the Backside 180° but without the pop.

THE kickass advice: if you wish to learn the rotation little by little, nothing is stopping you from starting off with a tilt of a few degrees and then jumping off the board. Of course only do this on a small ramp if you want to avoid twisting your ankle.

Axle Stall

Prerequisites: being comfy on the ramp and preferably knowing how to drop and be able to manage the end of this trick correctly.

What we can also call the 50-50 stall in a curve consists of blocking both trucks on the coping of the ramp and then going off in a normal position.

The placement of the feet is the same as for the Rock Fakie, or for a simple Ollie.

The trick step by step:

1. Gain some speed by going down another ramp, like an inclined one or a curve.
2. Go up the curve and once your nose goes above the coping rotate to 90° so that your back truck will block first and then you can block the second one on the coping
3. Slightly lean backwards to help maintain the balance and really place both trucks flat on the coping
4. You're now balanced, it's up to you alone to decide when to go off again seeing that you're maintaining the balance.
5. Now, press down on the tail and rotate to 90 ° towards the curve and then dive into it and slightly cushion the blow with your legs. Champion!

NB: Some skaters use the pelvis to go and lean backwards before the back trucks are even on the coping, it's another technic that you can try if you can't do it.

BS 5-O Grind

Prerequisites: Drop and the kick turn you must master young skaters (hear with Yoda voice).

I'd like to remind you that this is 5-0 but on a curve. If you're interested in this trick on a curb I have something for you and you'll find it in the Grind/Slide section.

The 5-0 is accessible to all and no other trick, apart from the drop, is necessary, also it can be learnt little by little.

How?

Simply by doing a kick turn at the top of the ramp! The kick turn is turning by using the tail, as I taught you above, both ways to turn with the board.
And so it's a very good introduction before really getting into the 5-0.

Just for you I'm going to break down the tips for this trick into **two parts:**

1. access version: the "grind" kick turn
2. The 5-0 grind with length

P1 - The trick step by step:

1. Your feet are in the same position as for an Ollie
2. You arrive near a curve with enough speed to be able to easily reach the top
3. Once your front truck goes above the coping push slightly on the tail all whilst turning with your pelvis and shoulders in backside direction. It's the exact same position as for a kick turn, the only difference being that it's at the top of a curve.
4. If you went high enough and gained enough speed your back wheel is supposed to go above the coping and your back truck should do a slight 5-0 grind. Don't be surprised by the slight tremble that this can bring and continue to do the rotation using your shoulders and pelvis without stopping to look at the birds.
5. Dive into the ramp again as if you just did a drop by slightly leaning forwards.
6. Go off with a smile on your face, you win!

P2 – Let's get serious!

Prerequisites: The "grind" kick turn helps a lot

The trick step by step:

1. Your feet are in the same position as for an Ollie or Kick turn
2. You go towards the curve with more speed than for a "grind" kick turn
3. Once the front truck is above the coping do a rotation using your pelvis and shoulders of only 90° in order to engage the back truck on the coping in grind.
4. Two things: Slightly lean back once the grind has been launched, so the truck is flat against the coping. And think about managing the balance of the 5-0, exactly the same as for a manual on the ground, it's as easy as that!
5. Don't hesitate to slightly swing your legs forwards to give them power and accelerate the grind on the coping
6. Once you've reached the end of the ramp, or if you want to stop, it's the same as for the kick turn, all you need is to redo a 90 ° rotation by slightly pushing on the board in order to unblock the truck and the wheel from the coping
7. Lean forwards all whilst cushioning the blow and you're off for another round!

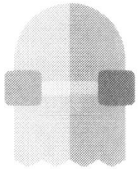

Feeble Stall

Prerequisites: The Axle stall, or at least the kick turn grind

Everything is done the same as for the axle stall except from the fact that instead of blocking the truck in axle (or 50-50) you'll put yourself in feeble. Meaning your front truck won't be engaged onto the coping but above it.

For those of you who still don't see what it looks like, go watch the video from the QR code above.

The feet placement still doesn't change, follow the same procedure as for the axle stall because everything is basically the same.

The trick step by step

1. You go towards the curve with enough speed so that your truck will go above the coping without effort
2. Once the truck has gone over the coping, do a rotation of less than 90 ° with your pelvis and shoulders (let's say 70-80° for the mathletes) in order to engage and block your back truck onto the coping
3. your front wheels and truck will lay on the flat edge of the ramp after the coping. This will give the board a diagonal orientation.
4. Slightly lean back in order to stabilize it all. In this position you'll be able to maintain the balance for as long as you

want to because the balance is well distributed, the same as for the Axle stall

5. To go off again push down onto the tail to lift the front truck and dive into the ramp

6. Slightly lean forwards, cushion the blow and go off towards new adventures!

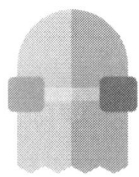

Bs/Fs Disaster

Prerequisites: Being comfortable on a curve, mastering the previous curve tricks, as well as the bs 180° and the fs 180° will help you GREATLY.

Disaster can be translated in French by Désastre or sinister. It's not the most dangerous trick, only the steeper your curve and the greater the danger. Let me explain.

The disaster consists in performing a 180° rotation at the top of a curve, to land in the other direction by stalling the rear truck on the coping (top of the curve often represented by a tube or a metal edge). You can just as well land on the middle of the skate and do a light boardslide, it's according to tastes and preferences :)

Procedure of the trick:
1. Drive fast enough towards the curve.
2. Position your feet as for a bs 180 if you want to do the bs disaster, or in fs 180 if you want to do the frontside version.
3. Climb the curve by starting to bend your knees, until your front wheels are very slightly before the coping.
4. Engage the rotation with the shoulders and the pelvis in the desired direction (fs or bs).
5. Land with the middle of the board, or just the rear truck locked at the top of the coping while cushioning with your knees so you don't lose your balance.
6. Lean very slightly forward to initiate the descent.
7. Go down and it's done!

Spinning at the top of the curve can be scary, feel free to start on the smallest curve available to you and even learn the move on a steep incline. The feeling will not be the same but can give you a good foundation for the future.

And after that ?

Like the previous tricks, you can add some salt to the disaster to make it even cooler. For example, you can add a revert when starting the descent. You can also add a flip, a bigspin, do it caballerial, boneless. Try :)

Grind section

First of all, before starting on rails of 30 steps I'll specify what a grind actually is.
The grind, which came to be in the 80' consists of "grinding" on a curve or even a rail. Meaning that your trucks will slide along the curb. It's not really that easy to explain so I think the next photo speaks for itself.

Doing a grind gathers a group of actions: to move quite fast, to do an Ollie, to land correctly on the curb/rail, grind and go off correctly with all four wheels on the ground (or not if you which to innovate)

The grind and slides offer new sensations to skaters, the same thing goes for the ramps and grabs.
Of course this takes training, you won't learn it just by snapping your fingers, same goes for all other tricks. So don't give up and start by learning the 50-50!

We'll start off by talking about the grinds and then the slides. However you're free to start by the slides if you wish to because the only base for the grinds and slides is the ollie.

Examples:

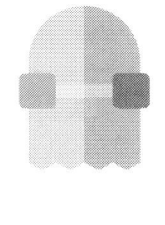

50-50

Prerequisites: Ollie as well as being comfy on your board.

The 50-50 is the basic grind to learn in skateboarding, this was the first true grind ever created.

To start off I would recommend a curb that isn't too high and preferably waxed. That way it's ready to welcome your trucks.

However, I would strongly advise against the rails. It isn't adapted for grinds but more for slides. It's still entirely possible to do a grind on a rail but a lot more dangerous for a beginner.

The trick step by step:

1. Move at a fast pace towards a curb or rail
2. Your feet are in the same position as for an Ollie
3. Try to align yourself at best with the curb in order to avoid having to do it later on. Try to be almost parallel to the curb.
4. Slam the ollie, all whilst being in the air you're going to align your trucks in a parallel position with the curb in order to place them on it when you land. The grind begins!
5. Slightly flex your legs in order to align your center of gravity in the middle of the board and gain balance.
6. Once you arrive at the end of the curb, slightly lift the back as if you were launching a manual.

7. Exit the curb, slam down and go off towards new adventures.

NB: The most difficult thing to learn is to really block your trucks properly on the curb.
Of course you can practise when you're still in order to learn the movement quicker and then correctly block your trucks. That's what I would strongly advise you to do first, before learning to do the trick while riding.

5-O

Prerequisites: The 50-50 grind is mandatory
A good balance in manual in flat can really help!

The step by step of the 5-0 is basically identical to that of the 50-50
Apart from the fact that only your back truck grinds on the curb and not your front one.

You can now understand why I would highly recommend having a good manual in flat to learn this trick. It's more than preferable.

The trick step by step:

1. Move at a fast enough pace towards the curb
2. Your feet are in the same position as for an Ollie
3. Slam the ollie and align yourself in a parallel position to the curb by putting more weight onto the tail.
4. If everything goes well you'll land in 5-0 thanks to the weight that you added towards the back.
5. Slightly flex your legs in the direction of the grind
6. Maintain the balance and get off once you've reached the end of the grind

The tip: Remember that everything is basically the same as for the 50-50, apart from the fact that you'll land on the back truck. Try to avoid scraping the tail too much on the curb, if the curb is waxed too much then you'll quickly do a faceplant.

Nosegrind

Prerequisites: 50-50 grind, the 5-0 is optional but can help to understand the balance in grind, that's why it's interesting to know it before trying to conquer the Nosegrind. You'll also need the nose manual to master the balance on both front wheels.

The nosegrind, along with the crook, is one of the more frequent tricks that you'll find in skateboarding videos. Once you've acquired the 50-50 and the 5-0, the nosegrind will be a lot more accessible. What you'll also find is a good grind sensation.
The nosegrind can reach a pretty neat aesthetic level, if on top you add a flip trick either at the start or the end, maybe even both.
The most common ones would be the nosegrind flip or even the nosegrind nollie fs 180° out.

The trick step by step:

The placement of the feet is still the same as for the previous grinds, EXCEPT that the front foot will gain a few centimeters towards the nose. This will ease the landing on the nose.

1. Ride quite quickly towards the curb
2. Slam the ollie and align yourself parallel to the curb by putting more weight onto the nose
3. Land softly on the curb with only the front truck
4. Slightly flex your legs in the direction of the grind
5. Maintain the balance by using your arms, the same as for the nose manual.

6. Maintain the balance until the end and exit with a little nollie flip (only joking, but why not!). A little push on the nose towards the front will do the job in order to exit without getting the back truck stuck on the curb.

The tip: Same as for learning the 50-50, before getting started I would advise that you learn a little thing that will really help you and open many doors for you.
Isn't that nice?

You'll learn to launch the nose manual after an ollie. To do so your feet are placed in the same position as for an ollie and the rest is done the same way. However, your front foot will scrape further down without coming back towards the middle of the board. The back foot follows the same scenario to finish your road near the 4 screws on the tail.

If you follow this to the letter, you'll easily land in nose manual and then it's up to you to manage your balance. Once you've acquired it, it will really help you for the nosegrind and of course, the nose manual on higher spots.

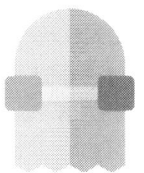

Crook

Prerequisites: the nosegrind

The must have of the grind! The same as for the nosegrind, the crook is very often seen in skateboarding videos. It's highly appreciated for its beauty as well as the sensation it brings. The same as for the previous grinds, it can be done on a curb as well as a rail.

Watch out to not confuse it with the over crook though, that we'll get to later on. The crook and the over crook are similar but not entirely the same, it's as if you compare the kickflip to the heelflip.

The trick step by step:

1. Move at a fast pace towards the curb, you must be facing the curb before launching the trick.
2. Place your feet in the same position as for a nosegrind
3. Slam the ollie, all whilst putting more weight onto the nose as I taught you previously in the trick tip.
4. As soon as you land on the curb, do a slight rotation to orientate the board towards the outside of the curb
5. Maintain the balance, always by using your arms
6. Once you reach the end, do the same exit as for the nosegrind.

NB: the trick is halfway between the Nosegrind and the Noseslide. The exit in Nollie 180° could help more than one.

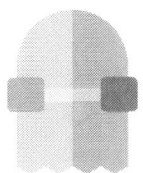

Overcrook

Prerequisites: the crook is mandatory and don't flinch!

As I previously said in the crook trick tip, the over crook is very similar. Only one thing changes, the orientation of the board during the grind. Instead of the truck being oriented towards the outside of the curb it's the opposite for the over crook, the truck is oriented towards the inside.

The trick step by step:

1. Move at a fast pace towards the curb, facing it.
2. Your feet are in the same position as for a crook
3. Slam the ollie, all whilst putting weight onto the nose, as I taught you in the advice for the nosegrind
4. As soon as you land on the curb, do a slight rotation to orientate the board towards the inside of the curb
5. The exit is the same as for the crook, normal, in 180° out, where you orient the nosegrind and do an exit in nollie. In my opinion it's the easiest if you want to concentrate on the grind.

NB: Watch out when you exit, decide in advance how you'll approach it.

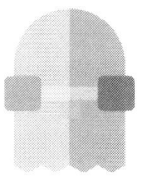

Salad

Prerequisites: the 5-0

Watch out, the salad is not an edible trick.
You can consider that it's the same as the crook but in the 5-0 version, because it's simply a 5-0 but oriented diagonally. Very nice, but unfortunately, it's being done less and less whether it be in skateparks or in videos. The nosegrind and crook are a lot more present.

The trick step by step:

1. Your feet are in the same position as for the 5-0
2. Move at a fast pace towards the curb
3. Slam the ollie
4. Do a slight rotation of the pelvis so the board is orientated towards the outside for the landing, or after having launch the 5-0, both solutions are possible
5. Block the back trucks on the curb and slightly move your center of gravity towards the back to give inertia.
6. Once you reach the end you can exit by doing the rotation from the start or go off in fakie by doing a fs 180 ° which can be sweet!

Slides

From now on we'll be doing tricks that are only based on slides. These are similar to grinds, only instead of sliding on the trucks, like for the grinds, you'll slide using different parts of the board.

This can be the middle of the board (boardslide or lipslipe), the tail (tailslide), the nose (noseslide) or even the grip (darkslide). That's how slides are done. Same warning as at the start of the book, go slow, because even slides can quickly throw you backwards or forwards.

Previously in the grind section, I mentioned that it was easier to do grinds on curbs. For the slides this isn't the case, because some slides will be easier to do on curbs and others will be easier to do on rails. Rest assured, I'll let you know when it's the case.

Right, let's stop messing around and get to training!

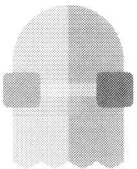

BS Boardslide

Prerequisites: the ollie, the fs 180° which can help you but is optional.

Type of spot: easier and more aesthetic on a rail

The boardslide is generally the first slide that you learn, because it's more accessible to all, the same goes for the 50-50 on the grinds.

Little reminder, still the same as for the 50-50, avoid the big spots to learn this trick. Find a small rail and not a guardrail. You'll probably find a small rail in your skatepark.

The trick step by step:

1. your feet are in the same position as for the ollie
2. ride at a fast pace with your back against the bar
3. Slam the ollie and do a 90° rotation in frontside (yes 90, half of 180 good sir)
4. The center of the board will now slide on the rail. Be careful not to lean too far forward or too far back. You need to lean very slightly backwards, not too much and not too little. It's up to you to find your own balance
5. Maintain the balance
6. Once you see the end, do a reverse rotation, meaning a backside 90°, to go back into the normal position

It's quite possible to go off in fs 90° to finish in switch.

NB: Preferably, do the trick on a low rail, and also for the exit to learn it correctly and lower the risk of early sterility!
You can also learn it with a slower pace, but remember that you still need speed, just try to avoid being retired before your time!
One thing that will really help you is to learn the trick when exiting the rail. This will help you learn it quicker, and once acquired you can start the slide earlier until you obtain the desired length.

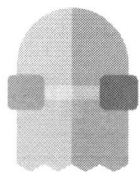

FS Boardslide

Prerequisites: In my opinion the frontside version is a bit more difficult, so I would recommend that you master the backside version before learning this trick

Type of spot: Rail

The trick step by step:

1. Your feet are in the same position as for an ollie
2. Move at a fast pace facing the bar, get as close as possible to it before launching the trick
3. Slam the ollie and do a 90° rotation in the backside. It's not a big deal if there are a few degrees less because the backside version is a lot harder
4. The center of the board must slide on the rail. Respect the balance between the front and the back in the same way as for the Bs Boardslide
5. When you see the end go in the reverse direction from the start, meaning a frontside 90°. Or add a backside 90° to go off in the switch.

The +: if you want to impress the gallery, while slamming the bs 90°, add a revert to cumulate 360° of rotation.

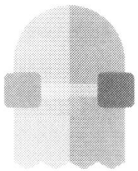

BS Noseslide

Prerequisites: Fs 180° and nothing else!

Type of spot: It's easier on a curb than on a rail.

The noseslide, along with the boardslide, is one of the most accessible slides for beginners.
Not because it has no other prerequisites than the fs 180° but because the movement of blocking the nose is a lot more natural than that for the tailslide or even the lipslide for example.
A waxed curb would be helpful.

The trick step by step:

1. Your feet are in the same position as for a frontside 180°.
2. You arrive with your back towards the curb at a moderate pace, not too fast, not too slow.
3. Slam the ollie and do a 90° rotation in frontside
4. The height of the ollie should be slightly higher than that of the curb
5. Only leave the nose above the curb, everything after that, including the truck, aren't part of the slide. The wheels will slide on the flat side of the curb.
6. Once you land on the curb you need to put almost all of your weight onto it. Then, maintain the balance between the outside and the inside of the curb: you shouldn't press too hard onto the nose or the back of the board
7. If all is well then the slide should launch

8. When you see the end, you need to give a slight push on the top of the board which will lift the weight off. Combine this with a 90° rotation in front, or in back, starting from the nose.
9. Slam down, cushion the blow and let's go!

Lipslide

Prerequisites: the boardslide will help a lot, it's basically mandatory for the lipslide

Type of spot: a rail, to make it easier to do a slide on the curb

The lip slide strongly resembles the boardslide, the only difference being that it happens before its launch.
Meaning that you have to slam an ollie in the opposite direction of the bar.
For example if you're facing the bar you'll do a fs 90° and you'll land a slide on the bar.
If your back against the bar, it'll be in backside 90°
And so we can say that the difficulty resides in the beginning and not during the trick, this goes for most skateboarding tricks.

As previously stated you can do this in front or back, here I'll explain the easiest version, meaning the frontside, facing the bar.

The trick step by step:

1. your feet are in the same position as for the ollie fs 180°
2. Move at a moderate pace facing the bar
3. Slam the ollie once your board is higher than the rail, turn your pelvis and shoulders to bring the board on the rail, the same as for a boardslide
4. The center of the board will now slide on the rail

5. Maintain your balance
6. Once the end is near you know what's left to do.

NB: the late rotation isn't easy to launch, you can also come slightly in a diagonal position in regards to the rail, which will reduce the rotation that needs to be done.
It's also possible to learn the rotation in flat without the rail. But don't present this in the skating game because it won't be valid. If courage is in your dictionary then you can learn the late Fs 180° in this way. All you need to do is to add the missing 90 °.

Frontside :

Backside :

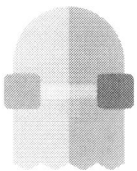

FS Tailslide

Prerequisites: the noseslide will teach you how to block and manage your balance, but knowing that the trick is done on the tail makes it optional to learn to obtain the tailslide
The frontside 180°, however, remains mandatory.

Type of spot: a curb, preferably waxed.

The tailslide is one of the harder slides but aesthetically one of the nicest. The same as for the previous tricks, I'd advise you to learn this trick on a curb that's quite low in order to limit the damage and also learn the movement slowly to start off with. It's very useful to learn how to block the tail first.

The trick step by step:

1. Your feet are in the same position as for the fs 180°
2. You arrive facing the curb at a moderate pace
3. Slam the ollie and do a 90° rotation in frontside.
4. Only leave the tail above the curb, everything after that including the truck aren't part of the slide. The wheels will slide (or not) on the flat side of the curb. This isn't mandatory, however, it can slow the slide down if the curb isn't waxed.
5. Once you land on the curb, maintain nearly all the weight on the tail. The same as for the noseslide, think about managing your balance.
6. Once you see the end, a few choices are available to you: exit in bs 180° or fs, flip, shove-it. Or to make it easier, give a slight push in backside to go off in the normal direction

7. Slam down, cushion the blow and congratulate yourself!

Grabs

The grabs are highly appreciated by skaters and highly recognised by non-skaters. Because they have probably seen Tony Hawk do a 900 on the tv or a child becoming famous thanks to his 1080.
Rest assured, I don't know anyone who knows how to do a 900 so it won't be in this book. But for your pleasure you can flash the below QR code in order to see both videos that I just mentioned.

The grind section that can be found here regroups all of the tricks where you grab your board. To make it clearer, grabbing your board is to touch or maintain the board with one or both hands. A variety of grabs exist from the classics, the tail grab or even Indy to the more difficult ones like the Benihana, the backflip and many more.

I'll present here, the grabs that are more accessible, meaning the easy level to the intermediate level.

The mythical 900 from Tony Hawk:

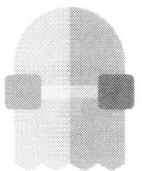

NoseGrab

The nose grab, for me, is the easiest grab to do. That's why I'm showing it to you here, and there are no prerequisites needed apart from the ollie of course, so get on your board!

You can do it in flat, so get on the floor the same as on a ramp and do an air for example. I'd advise you to learn it in flat first to really learn to slam the ollie and then grab the board.

For this trick your feet will be in the same position as for an ollie

The trick step by step:

1. move at a normal pace if you're in flat and at a fast pace if you want to do it in the exit of a curb
2. Once you're ready, or once you reach the top of the curb, slam the ollie with as much power as possible
3. Bend your legs as much as possible
4. Your right arm (for goody), and the left (for regular) will touch under the nose and maintain it. For this, you can slightly lean towards the nose to help you to maintain the board.
5. Once you start to go down, remove your hand from below the nose. And slam down softly
6. Cushion the blow using your legs and go off towards new adventures.

NB: In flat, the few seconds that you're in the air are counted, but it's a lot easier in order to learn the movement. Once the movement is acquired I would advise you to do it on a fun box, at the top of the curve to land on the flat end of the ramp. This type of ramp was especially made to do the grab.

Indy

Prerequisites: the nose grab, but this isn't mandatory. This can help you to learn how to bend your legs correctly and catch the board and then maintain it. A follow up of actions that are the basis of all grabs.

The Indy, the second most accessible grab and always so nice to do and to look at!
The nosegrind isn't a base for the Indy, but this one is easier because the targeted zone is the nose. So as you can guess, it requires less pop than the Indy, which has its grab zone in the center of the board.

For this trick your feet will be in the same position as for an ollie

The trick step by step:

1. move at quite a fast pace
2. Once you reach the top of the curb, slam the ollie with a maximum amount of power
3. Bend your legs as much as possible
4. Your left arm (for goofy), and the right arm (for regular), will touch the center of the slicing of the board to maintain it. Apart from bending down lower you won't be able to cheat like for the nose grab
5. Maintain your position by keeping straight
6. Once you start to lose height, remove your hand from the board. Slam down softly and cushion the blow.

NB: there is a similar trick that exists in Indy, the Mute, which is the same but with the other hand used while holding the board. You know what you have left to do.

TailGrab

This time the difficulty level is a little higher, not everyone will have the chance to be able to do this trick in flat on their first try because you'll need a good pop.
Therefore, if you don't want to waste any time, I would recommend that you go onto the ramp for the rest. It will help you to considerably increase your pop.

For this trick your feet are in the same position as for an Ollie

The trick step by step:

1. Move at a very fast pace towards the fun box

2. Once you arrive at the top, slam the ollie with the maximum amount of power that you can give

3. Bend your legs as low as you possibly can

4. Your left arm (for goofy), and the right arm (for regular) will touch the bottom of the tail and maintain it. For this slightly lean towards the tail to help to maintain the board, meaning towards the left for the goofy and the right for the regular. Be careful not to lean too much at the risk of laying back, which will cause you to fall at the landing.

5. Once you start to go down, remove your hand and slam down while cushioning the blow.

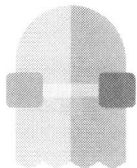

Nollie Tailgrab One-Foot

Prerequisites: A good nollie.

This trick is very nice and simple to perform especially if you have a good nollie with a good pop. The trick is to do a nollie, grab the tail of your skateboard and release the foot that has slammed the nose like a ninja! Well after you put it back on, that will save us from taking you to the hospital, ok?
Namely that you can perform this trick both flat and on ramps, like exiting an inclined plane for example, guaranteed effect!

Procedure of the trick:
1. Ride at a moderate pace.
2. The feet are positioned as for the Nollie.
3. Get down and smack the nollie hard.
4. Lean slightly towards the tail to grab it with your left (goofy) or right (regular) hand.
5. Naturally with the inclination, your front foot should take off, you just have to stretch it to have more effect.
6. Once you lose height, land while cushioning.
7. Cheer !

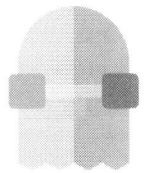

Melon

Prerequisites: the previous grabs to have a good base and especially the Indy

Info: non-edible

This is the hardest trick from this section. But rest assured there is an easier version that can be learnt first: the non-tweaked version.
The tweak in a grab is when you add, on top of the trick, a leg movement to give a stretch. Regarding the melon, the tweaked version will make you stretch out your legs completely in the air, which is really impressive but not easy to learn for a beginner. That's why it's best to learn the non-tweaked version (that I'll explain here) first.

For this trick your feet are in the same position as for an ollie

The trick step by step:

1. Move at the speed of light towards the fun box
2. Once you arrive at the top, slam the ollie with the maximum amount of power that you can give
3. Bend your legs as low as you possibly can to gain height
4. Your right arm (for goofy), and the left arm (for regular) will touch the back of the side of the board (between your two legs) and maintain it. For this you can slightly lean back. Be careful not to lean too much at the risk of falling back.
5. Once you start to lose the height, remove your hand from below the board, go back into the normal position and push the board back down slowly.

6. Cushion the blow and it's a win!

Special tricks
Old school

Because I want to make you happy and offer a maximum amount of tricks, whether you're a confirmed skater or a beginner I had the idea of adding this section.

For me, it's indispensable to all skaters who want to innovate a bit and stand out.

Highly appreciated by most skaters, old school tricks stand out for their originality as well as the fact that they are quick to learn compared to other tricks from the newer generation.

Moreover these will open up a lot more doors towards new tricks!

A very original skating game when choosing tricks:

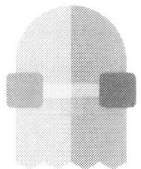

One Foot Manual

Prerequisites: A good balance, holding the Manual and/or the Nose Manual well can help you.

The One Foot Manual is the manual but with one foot. With the difference that it will be launched by the foot opposite to that of the classic manual. If you are goofy, your right foot will manage the balance of the manual and the reverse for the regular.

To throw it, nothing could be simpler, you put your foot which manages the manual on the skate, the heel will go on the tail and the front of the foot on the screws or shortly after.

Then we roll. Once you have enough speed, all you have to do is lift the unnecessary foot and apply pressure with your foot on the skate to press on the tail and then manage the front-to-back balance of the skate.

To land you can rest the 4 wheels on the ground or put the foot that was not on the skate on it to finalize the movement.

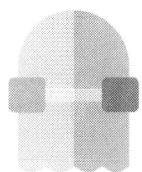

Boneless

The great Boneless! A simple trick that is accessible by all.

There are absolutely no prerequisites to gain access to this trick, not even the ollie, that's the beauty of it. Moreover, it can even be combined with many other tricks like the flips or even the shove-its. And of course, it's possible to gap steps in boneless!

For the feet placement, it's the same as usual, just look at your feet.

The trick step by step:

1. Move at a normal pace
2. Once you're ready, place your hands under your board near the middle
3. Wow, you look like a skater from the 60' in this position, classy!
4. Now it's going to be simple, you're going to remove your front foot from the board
5. You then place your foot on the ground, this will make the tail slam under your back foot
6. Rest on your foot that's on the ground to jump as high as possible whilst bending your legs and slam down in the air for even more class!

There you have it, it's done!

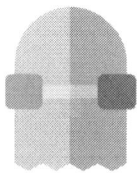

Boneless 180°

Prerequisites: the boneless helps but isn't mandatory

After the boneless, the 180° version can be learnt very naturally. Consequently the placement of the feet is the same as for the classic boneless.

The trick step by step:

1. Move at a moderate pace
2. Place your feet in the exact same position as for the boneless
3. Place your front foot on the ground, the tail will slam by itself thanks to the weight from the back foot
4. Turn your pelvis and shoulders towards the desired side, all whilst pushing down on the front foot to lift off, whilst being in the air continue the rotation using your shoulders and pelvis.
5. Really bend your legs, place your feet from the air on the board
6. Slam down softly and it's a success!

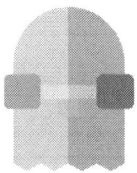

One Foot Nose Manual

Prerequisites: A very good balance, holding the Nose Manual well can be a positive point.

We saw the Manual and the Nose Manual together. As its name suggests, the One foot nose manual is a nose manual... with one foot. Just that. He's scarier and more visual than his little brother, of course. On the other hand, it is more difficult to hold than the nose manual, normal after all, isn't it?

For the positioning of the feet, it's a bit special. The front foot will go over the nose, perpendicular to the truck. It is the toes that will put pressure on the nose to lift the board and your heel that will balance backwards at the level below the screws. The back foot will not be used for much, you can place it on the 4 rear screws, we will come back to this below.

Procedure of the trick:

1 - Roll at a moderate pace, the same as for a nose manual.
2 - The feet are positioned as we said before.
3 - Remove your back foot and apply pressure to the nose using the front of your foot. The nose should sink and the one foot nose manual should be present.
4 - Maintain forward/backward balance to make the one foot nose manual last.
5 - When you want to land, you can put your foot back to lower the board, or you can give a slight push on the nose with your

front foot during the one foot nose manual to land and immediately put both feet back normally (prettier).

It's not an extremely complicated trick, it's all a matter of balance to manage.

209

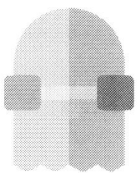

Boneless 360°

Now that you get how it works, we'll get into the harder part, the 360°! Enough to make you dizzy in a few seconds!
For the 360° version, everything is the same as for the 180° but only one thing changes : the way you do the rotation.

Prerequisites: the classic boneless and the 180°

The trick step by step:

1. your feet are in the same position as for a boneless 180°
2. Move at a moderate pace
3. Take the board and catch the tail all whilst starting to turn your pelvis and shoulders, a little before catching the tail
4. Now it's all in the shoulders, the pelvis and the thighs. To complete the 360° you need to "move" the movement forward with your thighs. Meaning that your thighs and pelvis will always be ahead of the rotation compared to the rest of the body.
5. If everything goes as planned, you'll land straight after having finished the last few degrees.
6. Slam down softly and cushion the blow

NB: If you can't finish the rotation entirely then finish it with a revert!

Don't hesitate to do the boneless in your own way by mixing it up with loads of different tricks!

Now that you are capable of doing the 360°, you can, for example, do a Boneless Big spin, Boneless Flip 360° and many others. Let your imagination run wild!

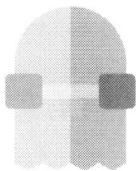

Cannonball and Cannonball 180°

Prerequisites: The cannonball has no prerequisites, for the 180° version it is of course preferable to master the classic cannonball. For the latest version, you will only need a good Ollie.

As the name suggests, this trick will turn you into a cannonball. Why ? Simply because you will be riding at a high speed, and your hands will be on the tail and the nose. Which has the effect of a cannonball in the air.

First version (normal and 180°):
For this one, the ideal is to do it on an inclined plane type ramp or a curve/funbox to land on the flat or leave in fakie.

It's extremely simple:
0 - Roll fairly fast towards an incline/skatepark curve.
1 - Place your feet on the eight screws.
2 - Put your right hand (left for regulars) on the nose, and the other hand on the tail. You will almost be sitting on the skateboard (without putting your butt down either). As if you were squatting on this one.
3 - Lower yourself to give impetus while pulling on your forearms to jump while lifting the skate.
4 - Here you are in full take-off, the hardest part is behind you.
5 - Land and leave for new adventures.

Here's a nice little trick to do in a skatepark without even having to know how to master the Ollie.

For the 180° the movement is completely the same except that you will add the rotation of the shoulders inwards (backside) or outwards (frontside).
Be careful, the movement will be less simple than a classic 180° in flat, simply because you will have much less room for manpower due to the low height. You will therefore have to be quick.

Second version (grabbed):
For this second version you can also do it on a ramp or even flat to start.
Rather than lifting the skateboard off the ground with the hands, here we will first perform an ollie and then put the hands down. Nothing extraordinary, don't worry.
1 - Ride at a moderate pace towards the incline or curve, or on the ground as desired.
2 - Position your feet as for an Ollie.
3 - Click the tail and scrape the grip with the front foot to then bend the legs as much as possible.
4 - While bending your legs to the maximum, lower yourself to put your hands under the tail and the nose.
5 - Hold the position, then remove your hands and land, cushioning correctly with your knees.

Here we are, now you have mastered all three versions. What largely adds spice in your panel of tricks and takes more pleasure in skating ;).

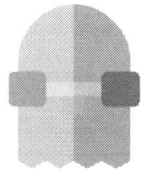

Pop Shove-it FS Revert

Prerequisites: the shove-it, obviously, as well as the revert

The shove-it revert is a very original trick that I highly recommend learning to have for your future game of skate. The sensation is also really nice!

The trick step by step:

1. Move at a normal pace
2. Your feet are in the same position as for a shove-it
3. launch the shove-it
4. When you slam down, land on the nose by hardly pushing down on it
5. With your pelvis and your legs do a revert in frontside
6. Continue to ride in Fakie

This is a really nice trick, the hardest part is to learn to land on the nose in order to immediately do the BS Revert. This requires a certain synchronization between your movements.

You can't learn to skate in the blink of an eye, so persevere!

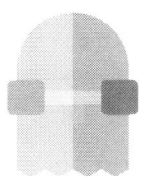

Disco Kickflip

Prerequisites: the kickflip and the body varial (explained below)

The disco flip is part of the more original tricks that everyone loves to do.
If you slam down during a skating game then your opponents will be completely lost.

The disco flip is actually a kickflip accompanied by a body varial
For those of you who don't know what a body varial is, it's actually a 180° rotation of your body without the board.

Meaning that on the board, you jump and turn 180°, to land in switch (or fakie if you prefer). For the disco flip, you'll do a frontside body varial, the same as for the ollie 180° front.

The trick step by step:

1. move at a normal pace
2. Your feet are in the same position as for a kickflip (see photos below)
3. Slam and launch the kickflip
4. Just after having launched the kickflip you need to do a 180° rotation only with the body
5. For this, it's all in the pelvis and shoulders
6. Normally you'll land in switch, soon after the board finishes its flip.

This trick is quite difficult to learn, it's the rotation that's the main problem.

For that, really think about jumping high and turn as fast as you can.

The secret: train yourself to correctly do a Body Varial without the flip to start with.

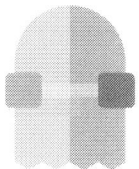

Powerslide

Prerequisites: the bs or fs revert are very important but not entirely indispensable

Always nice to do, the power slide gives a superb sensation of sliding if you compare it to a boardslide. The only issue with this trick is that you need a very smooth surface, like a varnished wood flooring for example. However it's possible to do the trick on a wet floor, or on smooth concrete. That's why you don't need to worry if you see your friends wet the floor with a gallon of water in the summer when it's 38°C out.

The power slide is a really cool trick. It's one of the many tricks that'll make you feel free. So what are you waiting for?

The trick step by step:

1. Move at quite a fast pace
2. Your feet are in the same position as for the revert, meaning the back foot on the tail and the front foot just before the nose
3. Start the trick by opening up your shoulders in frontside to force your pelvis and legs to follow
4. Put some power into your legs so that the wheels will slide on the ground and make a, roughly, 90° rotation
5. Slightly lean back to force the wheels to slide even more on the ground
6. Go back to the initial position by doing a revert in the opposite direction and go off in switch

NB: It's also possible to do it in 360°, all you need to do is put even more strength into your pelvis.

Fs No-Comply

Prerequisites: no trick is requested to learn the fs no-comply
However, it is preferable to really know how to ride your board

Seeing how you'll be slamming the trick in switch, it's not even imaginable to teach this trick to someone who doesn't know how to ride properly

The fs no-comply is part of the old school tricks, the same goes for the boneless, the fast plant, the bertlemann slide...
That's why it's really nice to have it in your list of tricks.
It's a trick that has a really nice effect in a line (line: follow-up of tricks) the same as for the 360° flip.
Moreover, it opens plenty of doors because it has many variants.

The trick step by step:

1. Move at a moderate pace
2. Your back foot is in the same position as for an ollie
3. The front foot is placed just above to the right of the top screws, before the nose. To make it simple: at the top right corner of the board, just not on the nose! Just before.
4. As you may have guessed, seeing as how it's in frontside, there'll be movement of the shoulders and pelvis that'll have to be completely synchronized.
5. Start by engaging your shoulders and pelvis in frontside and then let your front foot slide off your board.
6. this will force the back foot to slam the tail and at the same time slightly lift the board the same as for an ollie

7. Continue the movement in frontside with your shoulders and pelvis all whilst bringing the board along with the back foot
8. barely after having done 90° of the rotation with your board, remove your foot from the ground to finish the rotation in the air and then land with both feet
9. Go off chilling

At first glance it's a trick that isn't really that simple. A little advice to lighten the task would be to do the entire movement without jumping after 90°. This will enable you to learn the rotation correctly with your back foot to start off with.
In regard to slamming with your back foot don't hesitate to put power into it and assemble the movement with the rotation of the body.
The whole trick resides on these two factors.

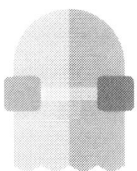

No Comply Fs Shove-it

Prerequisites: The no comply that we have seen before can help you and give you a good basis. Only, it is not mandatory, because you can do very well without it.

As you probably imagined when reading the title of the trick, it is a no comply, so launched with one foot, which will send a frontside shove-it that we even saw together in the flat section.

Personally, I find it even simpler than the No Comply Fs 180° because here only the board will turn, you will stay straight, apart from your legs which will move to launch the shove-it. Namely that you can do it both flat and on an inclined plane.

Procedure of the trick:
1. Ride at normal speed.
2. The feet positioned as for the fs no comply (it is the back foot that will do all the work of rotation).
3. Put the front foot on the ground, the tail slaps the ground. Jump lightly, resting on the foot on the ground. With the back foot, send the skate forward (your front, not the direction of the nose) by rubbing the tail.
4. The shove-it must launch, land once the rotation is complete.
5. Cheer !

Now that you have understood the principle, you can do no comply 360 shove it etc.

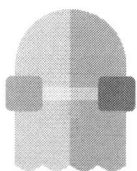

Bertlemann Slide

A unique and very old school trick!

The bertlemann slide is in fact a sort of power slide on the ramp, preferably a curb. Only this one is done with the hands.

No need for details, all you need is to go towards a ramp with speed and place your hands on it, putting weight towards the feet and then push down on them. The feet will do the power slide thanks to the hands that will do the rotation.

It's possible to this in 180°, 360°, 540°, etc

NB: if your wheels don't slide, don't hesitate to use wax or even water if you like the thrill. But DON'T EVER say that it was you and be prepared to hear from your friends who use the ramps for BMX.

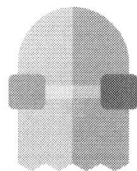

Old School Kickflip

The **only prerequisite** it has is the kickflip, but it isn't mandatory, as mentioned in the name it's old school and so that means that back in the day there were no kickflips!

Position your feet so that they make a right angle near the 4 screws on the tail. It's also possible to do this with both feet in a parallel position, it's up to you to choose which suits you best.

The steps of the trick:

Now it's going to get simple. Your front foot will give a push outwards which will start the kickflip, so 99% of the weight will go onto this foot. The other foot will launch the gesture by helping to lift the board so that the front will launch the kickflip. All you have left to do is to jump to the right for goofys and to the left for regulars.

The difficulty of the trick is in the rotation of the board. The higher you jump by bending your legs, the more time your board will have to turn. So, you need to really learn to do the launch of the trick with the front foot.

Annex 1

Choosing your skateboard

Choosing the board:

An important part that will concern beginners, as well as amateurs, because you can be completely comfy on your board even though it's not at all adapted to your size and/or style of skating.

For the size it's simple, the taller you are the longer the board you'll need. For example, for someone who is between 1.50m and 1.90m you'll need a board that is 7.5" to 8.5" max. Smaller boards are more for children and shorter people.

An important point that shouldn't be ignored: the wide boards are more for ramps, the same goes for wider wheels.

Choosing the grip:

When you buy a board in a skate shop or online, a basic grip will come with it (in most cases). This grip will do the trick so no need to go and buy a special one unless you like the drawing on this special one.

Choosing the wheels:

There are different advantages depending on the size of the wheels:
small: better acceleration in the thrust
wide: better on rough ground so goodbye to bad falls because of the little stones

A longer life expectancy has been observed with the wider wheels.

NB: rubber wheels make hardly any noise.

Choosing the trucks:

A whole panel of trucks exists, but the only thing you need to carefully choose is the width because the wider your board will be the wider the trucks will be!
So, watch out before buying.
The rubber from the trucks is also important, the softer they are the better you'll turn. You can also change them if ever they are too worn out. But rest assured they'll work just fine!

Choosing the bearings:

The bearings are divided into three classes: Abec-3, 5 and 7
The Abec 7 is the fastest.

NB: special mention for the swiss made bearings, they have a filter which stops the dust and all the small stones from getting in. But quality has a price!

Choosing the screws:

They are rarely sold with the trucks and have to be bought separately. They don't cost much and last (normally) a really long time. However the prices go up quickly if there is color on them, so it's up to you if this is indispensable on your board.

Annex 2

Game of Skate

Aaaaaaaaah the games of skate, don't you just love them. What would a session be without a skating game? Or an OUT.

It's true that it's fun, everyone shows off their own style to their friends, and that's where you can learn new tricks or give your competition, who didn't think you could do a switch big spin heelflip, a heart attack.

So for those of you who don't know it, the skating game, that you can also call skate or even OUT, are games that are played between skaters.

The principle: a dual between skaters, each for their own or in a team. The game starts with a rock-paper-scissors that will determine the order in which each skater plays. Once this is established, the first skater will launch a trick, whichever one he wants. And that's where the fun starts, the other skaters will have to repeat the same trick.

If a skater succeeds, he continues the battle. However, if he loses, he continues the battle (it wouldn't be any fun otherwise) BUT (yes there has to be one) he'll take THE LETTER. For example if your opponent can't do the trick he'll get an S from SKATE. He'll have 4 letters left to take before losing the round (S.K.A.T.E).

Of course the rules change, in France you'll have, in most cases, 3 tries to slam the trick, if you fail on the third try then you take a letter. In the US, the rules are a lot stricter and you only have 1 try for each trick (see The Berrics on the next page). Before dying you'll still have another try. In France you'll have 4 and in the US 2. It's up to you to choose which rules you like the most. If you allow old school tricks, hands, heels..

Regarding the OUT, it's like skate but with only 3 letters, so much quicker.

And look, you're never far from the smart guy that will always push further just to get another try in.

Special rules:

- **Add a redo**: ask to redo the trick. An interesting strategy to destabilize the opponent if he succeeds in a difficult trick that he does not fully master. In general, only one redo is assigned per player.
- **Number of additional attempts**: in order to progress and facilitate everyone's progress, before the game of skate do not hesitate to negotiate the number of attempts for each person. For example 4 tries for a beginner, reduce to 1 try for a confirmed.
- **Inversion:** A player pulls off a trick, but he uses his inversion to ask his competitors to pull off the trick in nollie or switch. Like the redo, only one per player as a rule.
- **The double/triple:** Like the +4 to the UNO, instead of performing the trick only once, players who must repeat the trick will have to perform it not once, but two or three times.
- **Body Varial:** Ask to add a body varial in progress, to the player who launched the trick or to his competitors.

Do not hesitate to use its special rules to spice up your game wisely. Whether it's for the player who has the hand, or for the skaters who reproduce his tricks so that it is equal. Don't hesitate to invent your own rules/bonus in order to have the most fun!

Now that you know about the skating games, what are you waiting for? Get out to your friends and try a bit!

One of the most impressive game of skates at the Berrics (Cody Cepeda Vs Luan Oliveira):

Annex 3
Having your own style or following the others?

Having your own style or following the others?

What we'll often notice in skateparks, or in the streets, is that there are two types of skaters: the one who innovates and the one who always learns other skaters' tricks.

In this section we'll see what the advantages and downsides are for both.

<u>The one that innovates</u>

Advantages:

the stagnation is practically unknown, he makes his own rules up and sets his own limits, this way he'll choose his own path and tricks in order to stand out from the others
Creates new tricks
More cards to draw in the skating game
The need to stand out and impress will result in a motivational growth

The downsides:

You'll often work on your tricks alone

A possibility of wanting to be a perfectionist

The one that follows

Advantages:

No need to think, you just follow the steps
Mutual aid between friends (or not)

The downsides:

you can stagnate seeing as you follow the progression of the "innovators" and they don't progress quickly
You might not always like the tricks, or they'll be at a lower level than yours (too easy/too hard).
The chances are equal to the skating game seeing as all your friends know how to do all your tricks

Follow or innovate is a choice that will entirely depend on your taste, and you. For example if you like to skate on your own with your music innovation is for you. However if you really like to skate with your friends, having fun and progressing a little slower, then the second rank is for you.

The best, of course, is a mixture of both. Then again you're free to do as you wish if you'd rather be one or the other.

Annex 4
The rider section

Finding wax easily:

A good plan for all skaters is to use anything that is greasy. Avoid anything like olive oil, it needs to be solid. Of course, the best thing would be to use candle wax, it's simple, effective and can be carried in your pocket. It's ideal for street sessions! I could have also shown you how to make your own wax but it's not really useful because to do so you need greasy products like paraffin and many others. You would have guessed it, it's a pain for nothing, a candle will do the trick just fine and you'll avoid a smack from your mum for having ruined her kitchen utensils. Moreover it's really quite cheap and I highly doubt you don't already have any at home! If you don't then go into any decoration shop, preferably buy flat-burning candles because they're easier to carry around in a backpack.

How to make your own skateboard rail and curb wax :

Foreword: Attention, the creation of wax is not without danger, for children/teenagers it is preferable to do it accompanied by an adult.

The wax is used to lubricate the support where the trucks/board will land for slider or grinder. It's essential for skateboarding and especially if you have curbs or slide bars that don't slip too much, especially on the streets for example.

Prerequisites: You will need a saucepan or frying pan, olive oil, candles or Babybel soap or wax. A mold that will be unusable afterwards: for example a can cut at the top (very sharp afterwards) will do the trick.

Making your skateboard wax step by step:

1 - Put a little water in the pan/saucepan so that the can floats.

2 - Heat over medium heat

3 - Once the water is hot and not checked by putting your finger in it, put the candles (without the aluminum!) or equivalent in the can.

4 - Take a utensil (cheap equivalent) to mix the candles which are starting to melt.

5 - Once melted, add a tablespoon of olive oil or butter.

6 - Mix. Turn off the heat/plate and let cool for a few minutes.

7 - Put the can with protective gloves in the freezer.

8 - Take out the bobbin after 30-40 minutes.

9 - Your wax is now ready! Cut the bobbin very carefully and take the wax out of the bobbin.

Repairing your shoes:

As mentioned at the beginning of the book, repairing your own shoes is a lot more economical than buying a new pair each month! A little example if you buy a new pair each month of roughly 50 (a quite decent pair) : 50x12 = 600. Yes you can check this all out, it comes up to 600. So as I said it's A CHOICE after all, if you can afford it then why not spurge a little but I'm not sure that everyone can. To repair your shoes two good products exist: the all-star gum and the shoe goo. Both are quite similar and you can find them for around a tenner in your local skate shop. I have also met a few skaters who use industrial glue. I can't recommend this because I don't know the origin or the brand but why not!

Caution, regarding the Shoe Goo: it's a product that has more chemicals and so is more harmful for your health (as indicated on the packaging). So I would recommend that you apply it in an open air area and preferably with latex gloves or any other gloves that will correctly protect you.

Replacing an old grip with a new one:

A grip can wear out quite quickly, with the water (unfortunate sessions that end under the rain), or even the ground and simply the wear and tear over time. That's why it's important to know how to change your grip. You can find a grip in your local skate shop or you can buy one online. The price generally varies between 5 and over 15 for higher end branded grips. And so it's ideal in order to increase the duration of your board. The only problem whilst replacing it is the glue. When putting on the grips you'll notice their power. As you may already know the true enemy of glue is the heat! Of course you won't be blowing on it so it dries, that might take some time, you won't be using petrol and a match. The easiest and quickest solution: the hairdryer. Place your board vertically and heat the top with a hairdryer for a few minutes. Once the grip is hot enough, you can unglue it from the top to the bottom without any trouble. Don't hesitate to use a Stanley knife to help you.

Re-thread your trucks:

Over time and the many flips performed, you accumulate slices and your trucks will take a big hit. You will surely realize this when you want to change wheels or change hardware on the trucks. Indeed, the thread (part of the truck where the nut is tightened), can be damaged and smoothed, which means that you will no longer be able to tighten your nut. Do not panic because you just need one thing, your hands and a skate tool and do as in the video below. That is to say, lay the skate tool flat and push the end of the truck into the end of the tool and turn gently to redo the thread. Be careful, lay the tool flat.

Do you need to place pads under the truck?

Pads, which are rubber/plastic rectangles can be placed under the truck, but what is their actual usage?
There are very few benefits but they are still worth the time:
→ Raise the board
→ "slightly" protect the board when you slam down by absorbing the vibrations.
→ For those who don't have a good ground to skate on, as the pads absorb the vibrations, it's more pleasant to ride on a rougher ground.

These are the only benefits to using them, so it's up to you to decide if it can be useful in your case.

Building a mini: https://www.youtube.com/watch?v=GyDNH07fl6A

How to learn almost all flat tricks without getting injured or falling?

You could believe in a technique or a miracle product from a guru or other fashionable influencer, but no, rest assured this is not the case.

First of all, I want to clarify that this technique is not valid for ALL tricks. All tricks containing body rotations are not affected. Now, let's talk a bit about technique and equipment.
For this, you will need a barrier or an equivalent, such as the high barriers of skatepark ramps. The only rule to remember

when choosing your spot is the height. Indeed, the barrier must be of sufficient size so that you can stand up and put your hands on it while jumping.
You understood ? It is used to stabilize you when learning a trick. This means that you can land any way, even in a slice and you will not run any risk. Simple and effective, this technique allows any skater to learn the most complex tricks: hardflip, inward heelflip, nollie versions...

Another very slight downside: 360° tricks like the 360° flip, or the lazer flip. These are tricks that require a lot of room to be sent correctly. It will therefore be slightly more complex to place them in a limited space.

Now that you understand how it works, it's up to you to have fun learning the most complex tricks as well as all the variations of late shove-it and flips.
Have fun !

Example of learning Hardflip with the help of a skatepark barrier:

242

Annex 5
Jump higher and improve the height of your tricks, is it possible?

Luan Oliveira, as well as other skaters, have distinguished themselves by an ability to pop their tricks higher than the norm. Indeed, if you watch the videos from Luan Oliveira or his matches in the Battle At The Berrics, his pop will jump out at you. No matter the trick, Luan takes off so high that you might wonder if he has springs instead of his soles.

Improving your jump is of course possible, however, it remains impossible to defy physics. By performing these exercises you can of course gain a few centimeters. Add to that an execution of the technique to perfection, and you will be the new Luan Oliveira!

How to improve your jumping technique?

As to improve your ollie, to take off a kickflip or any other trick there is no mystery: you just have to bend your legs before throwing the trick and then keep them bent in the air. Everything is on impulse, if you do the maximum in the preparation, as in full jump you can only improve the height of your trick. No wonder, do an ollie by bending your knees only a few centimeters, then do another one by bending them as much as possible in both phases. You will see the second version will naturally be taller.

How to improve the height of your jumps?

Here, we now start from the fact that you take off at your maximum: you bend your legs when throwing the trick, as well as in height. So you are doing the best you can. Now, we are going to see how you can work on the various factors that will make you able to take off even higher!

What areas should I work on?

1. To improve its jump height we must play on speed and strength in order to perfect explosiveness and plyometrics.

2. To increase your flexibility, stretch (see dedicated chapter) if you want to go as high as possible.

3. Do not exercise every day, leave at least one day of rest between each session. For each exercise try to do 2 to 5 sets of 6 to 12 repetitions, it will be more than enough.

Let's move on to exercises to improve your jump:

The warm-up:

First of all, before doing the exercises, take the time to warm up the following joints: pelvis, knees, ankles.

To improve strength and explosiveness: squats and/or lunges and/or deadlift.

To improve your speed: sprints (intervals for example) and/or jump rope.

Both while working on your jump: jump squats.

The Roman chair exercise can also be interesting.

The stretches:

For stretching at the end of the session, take the time to stretch your hamstrings and quadriceps muscles.

Do not hesitate to flash the QR codes to learn the method to perform each of the exercises:

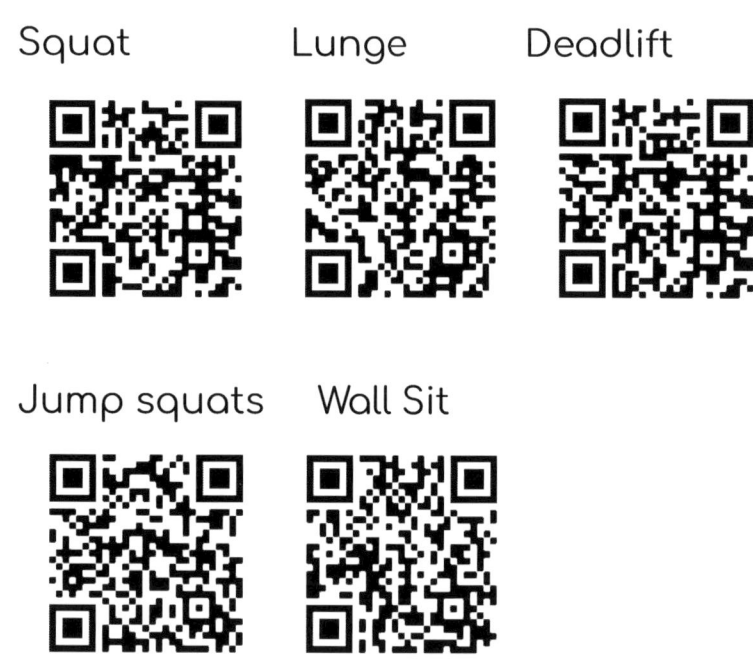

Annex 6
About the author

The idea of writing this book came to me when I started seeing a lot of people trying to figure out how to do a precise trick. In France there aren't many tutorials / lessons to learn skateboarding, there are mainly only American videos.

Why a book?
We might be in the XXI century but for me a paper book will forever be, to this day, better than the digital one in order to learn something. Along with videos it's ideal.

More street or park?
Honestly both, you get two different sensations when doing both.

The future of skateboarding?
I'd like it to be more known, without falling into excessive media coverage. Skating and it's life philosophy is quite liberal nowadays and that doesn't need to change.

Your favorite trick?
I don't have one single one, but without a doubt the One Foot nose manual, half cab heelflip, no-comply fs 180° and the cab.

Advice for beginners?
Really understand the basics almost to perfection, and then afterwards innovate and try new things to have fun. And of course don't give up, it's hard at the start but the harder you work on your tricks the better you'll get. Some are harder than others, that's the beauty of it. If there wasn't a challenge it wouldn't be any fun.

Annex 7
A few cool links

My favorite website:
http://www.thrashermagazine.com/

My skate app on Android :
https://play.google.com/store/apps/details?id=dfmv.skatetricks&hl=fr

My skate app on iOS :
https://apps.apple.com/us/app/skate-tricks/id1478881964#?platform=iphone

Nice skate videos :
https://skateboarding.transworld.net/

Game of skate and other videos :
https://theberrics.com/

And of course YouTube that contains millions of videos about skateboarding.

My favorite Youtube channels:

https://www.youtube.com/c/thrasher: The world of skateboarding, the latest videos, the king of the road (not for a few years but it was great), and many more.

https://www.youtube.com/user/TransworldSKATEmag: Like Thrasher, a must have.

https://www.youtube.com/c/berrics: The Berrics channel, surely one of the best in the world to follow with that of Thrasher.

https://www.youtube.com/c/JonnyGiger/videos: A golden skater who pushes the limits of flatland tricks, I love his channel.

https://www.youtube.com/channel/UCP94Q0ypuPdhl-NupoAbcoQ/videos: gear, test and many more. Ben always treats!

https://www.youtube.com/chrischann/videos: Chris Chann, another great skater to follow.

https://www.youtube.com/c/thenineclub: The Nine club, very interesting podcasts with pro skaters.

https://www.youtube.com/c/RadRatVideo/videos: Rad Rat, another great channel.

Chris Haslam and Daewon Song (two of my favorite skaters) are very present on Instagram, I really like their style but unfortunately they don't have a YouTube channel. However you can find their videos on YouTube by typing their names.

Annex 8
Skate Tricks app & blog

Skate Tricks is an app designed by skateboarders and for skateboarders! One wonders who came up with the idea for this awesome project ... so find out ... The app is available for Android and iOS.

Features:

- Tricks: classified from easy to extreme level, you will find all the tricks here, including the most original. Some new tricks are added over time through updates to the app.

- Game of Skate: as the name suggests you can play Game of Skate with your friends. If you don't know how to play it, or if you've forgotten, don't hesitate to go to Annex 2.

- Dice (Skate Dice for aficionados): A great way to train while having fun, alone or with others, it allows you to challenge yourself by throwing a random trick. Then it's up to you to prove yourself. Filters have been added, allowing to filter the level of difficulty of the tricks but also the category.

- Skate School: quite similar to dice, but in a different form. The Skate School offers to learn one trick a day, no more, no less. Here no filters, no frills, only the name of the trick which changes every 24 hours. This leaves you plenty of time to learn the trick in question or perfect it!

- Profile: the profile is full of very interesting features: statistics such as tricks learned, those remaining, trophies won etc. You will also find in the profile the list of trophies, his collection of successful tricks, his customizable photo and much more.

As you can see, I decided not to put screenshots of the app. This is constantly evolving and changes a lot to please the greatest number.
So you know what you have to do if you can't wait to see this awesome project and want to have a blast on your own or with your friends. The app is free and available for iOS and Android :

Besides that, I invite you to visit the blog of the application where you can find additional content, be it trick tips, advice, materials, news and many others.
Available at this address:
https://dfmv.xyz/skate-tricks-app-us/index.php

Annex 9
Glossary
(don't worry, there's no shame in being here)

Goofy: the skater kicks with the left foot and the right foot is at the top of the board. After the kick the left foot is placed on the back of the board.

Regular: the skater kicks with the right foot and the left foot is at the top of the board. After the kick the right foot is placed on the back of the board.

Switch: It's to ride in the opposite position, if you're a goofy you'll ride in regular. For more detail, see the stance section.

Mongo: this defines the skaters that are neither a goofy or a regular. The foot that is on the board is placed at the back and he kicks with the foot that is supposed to be placed on the top of the board. You'll probably meet skaters that skate like this. If this is the case for you, and that you wish to change it, place your foot at the front of the board instead of the back and get used to this.

PS: the mongo skaters are seen as lefties from the middle ages.

Mall Grab: holding your skateboard by the truck when walking. A practice banned by some skaters. A facebook page exists where you can see skateboarders holding their skateboards like this. Like Thrasher t-shirts or Vans, they have gradually become markers of "poses", to which we must understand a person who adopts the style of the skater in its entirety without knowing how to ollie. Of course it's all humorous, although some people take it too seriously, but that's another topic.

Tail: the part of the board where you place your back foot. It's with the tail that you do an ollie for example or even a manual.

Nose: The front part of the board. This is where you'll do a nollie or even a nose manual for example.

"One more try": when you do a skating game it's the expression used to designate an additional try or when you ask for one.

Tricks: a "figure" in skateboarding, for example the kickflip. This term designates all the figures, whether it be an ollie, the hardflip or even the manual.

Old school: Designates the old school of skateboarding, the old style with the boneless, no complys...

New school: these are all the other tricks that appeared after the Rodney Mullen period: flips, grinds.

The skate game/OUT: game between skaters you can see the rules in the section of the same name

Handrail: rail on a set of stairs, you need to be ready before skating on rails because it's not without risk.

Gap: This is when you jump several steps in ollie for example. You can say to gap stairs or a bloc. "gap a set of stairs in flip..."

Grind: A grind is when the trucks of the board slide along a curb or a rail, for example when you do it in 50-50. Not to be confused with the slides.

Slides: when one of the parts of the board slides against the curb or the rail, this can be the nose, the tail or even the center of the board. For example; boardslide, noseslide or even tailslide.

Grab: The grabs belong to a category of tricks where you touch or maintain the board with one or both hands. For example, the Indy grab.

Coping: This is the tube at the top of a curb where you can grind, slide or even do tricks in a static position like the axle stall or even the rock fakie.

Wax: product used to lubricate a curb or rail if it isn't slippery enough to be able to do a slide or grind. You can also use it on inclined planes to do power slides from the future (watch out this is dangerous for BMX and scooters)

Module: Skating ramp

Street: the street in which you skate in spots that are completely natural, that haven't previously been used for skating. For example, a set of steps, a bench, a square...

Spot: Element that isn't initially planned but entirely skatable. For example, the benches in front of the station, steps in town ... You can also use this term to designate a skatepark.

Skate park: usually built with ramps, pyramids, fun box, ledges, mini and also street: rails, curbs

Street park: the same as for the skatepark but more street oriented. Meaning there will be more steps, rails or even inclined planes as well as many curbs.

Contest: skating competition

Line: a follow up of tricks. Whether it be in flat, grind, slide or even grab.

Bs: backside

Fs: frontside.

Skate tool/Tool: "Hey man, don't you have a tool?" Don't panic, we just ask you for the T-shaped tool that allows you to tighten all the screws on a skateboard. Around 10-20€ but will save your life several times over, and not just yours.

"This is the end, my only friend the end" - The Doors

Here resides the end.

I thank you, the reader, to have taken the time to read this book. I sincerely hope that you liked it, because I've made it with all my heart. If you want to thank me for my work, don't hesitate to leave a good comment on Amazon. This could help me a lot and allow other people to discover my book. Know that there is no age to skate, you can stop in your twenties because of school, but don't stop because someone tells you it's for kids. Either way you'll get back on it eventually, why? Because skateboarding isn't a sport, it's much more. It's a lifestyle, a religion. Once you're in, you're in.

Printed in Great Britain
by Amazon

14859771R00148